LANGUAGE AND LITERACY SERIES

Dorothy S. Strickland, FOUNDING EDITOR
Celia Genishi and Donna E. Alvermann, SERIES EDITORS

(Continued)

For volumes in the NCRLL Collection (edited by JoBeth Allen and Donna E. Alvermann) and the Practitioners Bookshelf Series
(edited by Celia Genishi and Donna E. Alvermann), please visit www.tcpress.com.

teaching**media***literacy*.com:
A Web-Linked Guide to Resources and Activities
RICHARD BEACH

What Was It Like? Teaching History and Culture Through
Young Adult Literature
LINDA J. RICE

Once Upon a Fact: Helping Children Write Nonfiction
CAROL BRENNAN JENKINS & ALICE EARLE

Research on Composition
PETER SMAGORINSKY, ED.

Critical Literacy/Critical Teaching
CHERYL DOZIER, PETER JOHNSTON, & REBECCA ROGERS

The Vocabulary Book: Learning and Instruction
MICHAEL F. GRAVES

Building on Strength
ANA CELIA ZENTELLA, ED.

Powerful Magic
NINA MIKKELSEN

New Literacies in Action
WILLIAM KIST

Teaching English Today
BARRIE R.C. BARRELL ET AL., EDS.

Bridging the Literacy Achievement Gap, 4–12
DOROTHY S. STRICKLAND & DONNA E. ALVERMANN, EDS.

Crossing the Digital Divide
BARBARA MONROE

Out of This World: Why Literature Matters to Girls
HOLLY VIRGINIA BLACKFORD

Critical Passages
KRISTIN DOMBEK & SCOTT HERNDON

Making Race Visible
STUART GREENE & DAWN ABT-PERKINS, EDS.

The Child as Critic, Fourth Edition
GLENNA SLOAN

Room for Talk
REBEKAH FASSLER

Give Them Poetry!
GLENNA SLOAN

The Brothers and Sisters Learn to Write
ANNE HAAS DYSON

"Just Playing the Part"
CHRISTOPHER WORTHMAN

The Testing Trap
GEORGE HILLOCKS, JR.

Reading Lives
DEBORAH HICKS

Inquiry Into Meaning
EDWARD CHITTENDEN & TERRY SALINGER, WITH ANNE M. BUSSIS

"Why Don't They Learn English?"
LUCY TSE

Conversational Borderlands
BETSY RYMES

Inquiry-Based English Instruction
RICHARD BEACH & JAMIE MYERS

The Best for Our Children
MARÍA DE LA LUZ REYES & JOHN J. HALCÓN, EDS.

Language Crossings
KAREN L. OGULNICK, ED.

What Counts as Literacy?
MARGARET GALLEGO & SANDRA HOLLINGSWORTH, EDS.

Beginning Reading and Writing
DOROTHY S. STRICKLAND & LESLEY M. MORROW, EDS.

Reading for Meaning
BARBARA M. TAYLOR, MICHAEL F. GRAVES,
& PAUL VAN DEN BROEK, EDS.

Young Adult Literature and the New Literary Theories
ANNA O. SOTER

Literacy Matters
ROBERT P. YAGELSKI

Children's Inquiry
JUDITH WELLS LINDFORS

Close to Home
JUAN C. GUERRA

Life at the Margins
JULIET MERRIFIELD ET AL.

Literacy for Life
HANNA ARLENE FINGERET & CASSANDRA DRENNON

The Book Club Connection
SUSAN I. MCMAHON & TAFFY E. RAPHAEL, EDS., ET AL.

Until We Are Strong Together
CAROLINE E. HELLER

Writing Superheroes
ANNE HAAS DYSON

Opening Dialogue
MARTIN NYSTRAND ET AL.

Just Girls
MARGARET J. FINDERS

The First R
MICHAEL F. GRAVES, PAUL VAN DEN BROEK, &
BARBARA M. TAYLOR, EDS.

Talking Their Way into Science
KAREN GALLAS

The Languages of Learning
KAREN GALLAS

Partners in Learning
CAROL LYONS, GAY SU PINNELL, & DIANE DEFORD

Social Worlds of Children Learning to Write
in an Urban Primary School
ANNE HAAS DYSON

Inside/Outside
MARILYN COCHRAN-SMITH & SUSAN L. LYTLE

Whole Language Plus
COURTNEY B. CAZDEN

Learning to Read
G. BRIAN THOMPSON & TOM NICHOLSON, EDS.

Engaged Reading
JOHN T. GUTHRIE & DONNA E. ALVERMANN

Reading
Girls

The Lives and Literacies
of Adolescents

Hadar Dubowsky
Ma'ayan

Foreword by
Margaret Finders

Teachers College, Columbia University
New York and London

Published by Teachers College Press, 1234 Amsterdam Avenue, New York, NY
10027

Library of Congress Cataloging-in-Publication Data

Ma'ayan, Hadar Dubowsky.
Reading girls : the lives and literacies of adolescents / Hadar Dubowsky
    Ma'ayan ; Foreword by Margaret Finders.
      pages cm. — (Language and literacy series)
    Includes bibliographical references and index.
    ISBN 978-0-8077-5314-9 (pbk. : alk. paper)
    ISBN 978-0-8077-5315-6 (hardcover : alk. paper)
      1. Adolescence. 2. Literacy—Social aspects. 3. Junior high school girls—
    Attitudes. 4. Educational sociology. I. Title.
    LB1135.M27 2012
    302.2'244—dc23   2011045485

ISBN 978-0-8077-5314-9 (paperback)
ISBN 978-0-8077-5315-6 (hardcover)

Printed on acid-free paper
Manufactured in the United States of America

19 18 17 16 15 14 13 12 8 7 6 5 4 3 2 1

This book is dedicated to all the marginalized girls who are searching to be heard.

Contents

Foreword

In recent years, educational issues have captured the attention of most of the nation. Many of us closely follow the actions of politicians and educational policies that seem to vilify teachers and blame learners. With the current educational policies, all we seem to get is more of the same. It hasn't worked, and it isn't working. How can we improve educational opportunities for all learners? Rather than listen to divisive policies that may privilege one group over another or media rhetoric that has ground down teachers' morale and corroded public confidence in our schools, we need to listen to educators and scholars like James Gee and Allan Luke and Ernest Morrell and Marc Lamont Hill and Jabari Mahiri—and Hadar Dubowsky Ma'ayan. The inequities in schools have never been greater; they are more segregated racially and economically. At a time when class sizes are soaring, at a time when test scores become the hallmark of school success, at a time when money flows into the privatization of schools, at a time when teachers are vilified and children are blamed, we need to listen to educators like Ma'ayan who in this book brings to life the youth whom current laws and policies ignore. The rhetoric currently circulating in the media and in government-policy documents conceals the wealth of resources that diverse students and their families bring to school and to literacy learning. If you are reading this book, you know that the problem is not youth. The problem is not teachers.

When I learned that Hadar Ma'ayan viewed her work as an updated extension of *Just Girls: Hidden Literacies and Life in Junior High*, I was flattered and appreciative. Important understandings in the field of adolescence and literacy have developed since the 1997 publication of my book. *Just Girls* was followed by a number of books and research articles that address the many facets of adolescents' complex lives. Ma'ayan's work joins those important books.

Practitioners and researchers who work with adolescents express a growing concern that federal and state legislation that focuses attention on early reading programs will divert attention from the needs of adolescents and reduce expanded definitions of literacy. While much of the current literature on adolescent literacy has been expanding definitions of literacy to include reading, writing, viewing in multiple contexts in and out of school, with print and nonprint texts, some of the most recent work seems to be narrowing the field. Literacy is often reduced to reading, and reading reduced to in-school reading. What is needed are more studies of adolescents engaging in literacy practices in multiple contexts, studies in school and out to determine what instructional practices and infrastructures would best support adolescents engaged in literacy in multiple contexts with multiple tools. Ma'ayan's book does just that.

Hadar Ma'ayan's work is important at this historical moment when schools are under siege. When most of the attention is on standardized testing and in some cities literacy instruction has become scripted, the teacher is still important. The learner is important. Ma'ayan pushes us to see real students and to create learning experiences that connect to their lives.

In this book, the author introduces us to six early-adolescent girls and allows them to speak for themselves. Through their experiences, Ma'ayan addresses the nature of contemporary youth culture influenced by the digital age. In a highly engaging and accessible manner, she allows us a window into embodied gender performances and includes multiple forms of literacy, including visual and technical, which extend the range and technical integration of multimodal communication. New literacies and multimodal literacies pose tremendous challenges to educators to rethink literacy in productive ways and to restructure their pedagogies to respond constructively to the technological and social changes we are now experiencing.

At the same time that technological advances shape youths' literacy experiences, many education policies are constricting rather than expanding literacy pedagogy. At a time when educational policies seem to ignore the rich literacies that youth bring to school, Hadar Ma'ayan shows how schools and literacy pedagogy need to change in this new era to better accommodate and build on new literacies that are the very core of experiences for many contemporary youth. We need to listen.

—Margaret Finders, University of Wisconsin-La Crosse
Author of *Just Girls: Hidden Literacies and Life in Junior High*

Acknowledgments

I would like to thank my mentors at the University of New Mexico for inspiring me and keeping me on track: Kathryn Herr, Elizabeth Noll, Ann Nihlen, and Nancy Lopez. I also gratefully acknowledge my colleagues who read my writing and offered feedback in the early phases: Frances Ortega, Marc Davidson, and Susan Calloway. I owe much to my fellow teachers at "Lincoln Middle School," especially "Ms. Carpenter," who allowed me to enter her classroom and was strong enough to be vulnerable enough to let me study her students and practice.

I have wheelbarrows of gratitude for my all of my mother friends—especially Patty Dexter, Nikki Hoffman, and Elizabeth Miller—who offered childcare, camaraderie, and a few cocktails along the way. Above all, I acknowledge Dina Ma'ayan, keeper of my heart, who supports me in all of my journeys, including this one. And, of course, my three children: Rafael, Samuel, and Lilith, who keep my heart open, honest, and giving.

I would like to thank all of the young people I have worked with over the years and whom I work with today, in classrooms, afterschool programs, summer camps, and Youth Enrichment Services. You inspire me to rise to the challenge, each and every day, of making my life a blessing and working to make a contribution in healing this sometimes broken world of ours. Finally, I offer thanks to the girls of the Girls Literacy Discussion Group who let me peer into their lives with grace and trust.

Introduction

My inside self and my outside self
Are different as can be.
My outside self is very thin,
She doesn't look unique,
She always seems to blend right in,
Afraid of what she seehs,

My inner self is different
Even though you cant see,

My inner self is full of colors,
Full of personality,
she dreams of far off places,
Different just like me

Inner
self

Poem and Drawing by Moniqua Nassim, age 13

There are over 3 million girls enrolled in urban public schools across the United States. Moniqua Nassim is one of these girls. She attends Lincoln Middle School, a public middle school in one of the nation's largest school districts.

This book focuses on six adolescent girls, including Moniqua, at a public middle school. At first glance, girls appear to be doing better in school than boys. Studies from the last decade indicate that girls graduate from high school and college at higher rates than boys, their grade point averages are higher than boys', and they are less likely to be expelled or held back. However, academic achievement—as defined by standardized test scores, grade point averages, and drop-out rates—does not tell the whole story of how girls and young women fare compared to boys and young men. According to the Institute for Women's Policy Research (2011), overall, women still earn less than men in every occupation, and poverty rates are higher for women in every racial and ethnic group. Full-time working women still make only 77 cents for every dollar that a man makes, and these rates are worse for women of color, with Hispanic women making only 53 cents for every dollar a White man makes. Women are more likely than men to be victims of physical and sexual violence (U.S. Department of Health and Human Services, 2011) and are still sorely underrepresented in government offices (National Foundation of Women Legislators, 2011), higher paying occupations, and corporate leadership (Institute for Women's Policy Research, 2010).

Middle school is a critical time in the lives of young women. In many ways, middle school is a gateway for academic and vocational success. At this time, students are navigating construction of identities, which includes developing narratives about who they are as students, where they will be in the future, which paths are open to them and which paths are closed. In the U.S. public school system, middle school is often the beginning of overt tracking of classes, such as leveled math or language arts. This academic differentiating of core classes increases in high school, opening doors for some students and closing doors for others. Middle school is a space of liminality; students enter at age 11, as children or tweens, and leave at age 14 as young teenagers on their way to becoming young adults.

As Moniqua describes above, middle school students are navigating their inner and outer selves as they construct identities, which include facets such as race, class, sexuality, and gender expression. As part of this construction of self, they use the texts they come across in their lives. They engage with texts as they read them to find themselves in the world. Middle school girls use multiple texts and literacies to understand themselves as young women.

This book provides insight into how middle school girls use the multitude of texts in their lives to make sense of themselves in the world. Students today live in a text-saturated world. The literacy practices that occur in school are only a fraction of the daily literacy practices of middle school students today. In the first half of the 20th century, books, film, radio, and newspapers were the primary texts to which children had access, and even those were limited. Beginning in the early 1950s and continuing through the end of the century, children's media experiences expanded to include television and now cable and satellite channels, recorded music, video, electronic games, interactive digital texts, and the Internet. President Barack Obama (2009) noted this significant shift:

> Every day, we are inundated with vast amounts of information. A 24-hour news cycle and thousands of global television and radio networks, coupled with an immense array of online resources, have challenged our long-held perceptions of information management. Rather than merely possessing data, we must also learn the skills necessary to acquire, collate, and evaluate information for any situation. This new type of literacy also requires competency with communication technologies, including computers and mobile devices that can help in our day-to-day decision making.

I came to my research as a middle school teacher with 5½ years of classroom teaching experience, 2½ of those at Lincoln Middle School. I took a break from classroom teaching to expand my knowledge of how students learn. I chose to return to the school where I had taught and would possibly teach again because I believed it was the best place to investigate the issues that had intrigued me as a classroom teacher.

After spending hundreds of mornings watching students flow in and out of my classroom, I wanted to better understand the experiences of these students, a venture that I never had time for as a classroom teacher. After spending years teaching literacy, carefully selecting texts, and creating assignments, I wanted to understand what role literacies play in students' understandings of self and how we, as educators and parents, can use literacies to help girls, especially those marginalized in school, to build resiliency, self-agency, academic achievement, and personal growth.

For me, the experience of practitioner action research was an incredibly powerful one. "Doing classroom research changes teachers and the teaching profession from the inside out, from the bottom up, through changes in teachers themselves. And therein, lies the power" (Bissex & Bullock, 1987, p. 27). This study allowed me to meet with a group of six students at a time, once a week, in a Girls Literacy Discussion Group. As a classroom teacher, I would never have had that time with a small group of students. The Girls Literacy Discussion Group became not only a site of research data collection but also a learning space for the participants and an eye-opening educational experience for me as a teacher. The implications from this study are significant because they are rooted in naturalist inquiry, a real-life experience of a teacher and students working together to make meaning.

For almost an entire school year I followed these girls. I met with them weekly as a group during their language arts period. I spoke with them individually, observed them in class and during free time, and collected artifacts from their school day. Throughout the course of the research, I asked the girls what they liked to read, watch on TV, search on the Internet, listen to on the radio, and watch in the movie theaters. I asked them how they felt or made meaning of texts that were given to them. We discussed texts such as their science books, math class assignments, church sermons, advertisements, song lyrics, e-mails, text messages, teachers' lectures, novels, personal drawings, and poetry. I asked them which texts were most significant to them and which they felt made a real difference in their lives. I inquired about their experiences with learning, their relationships with others, and their future plans.

I came to find that the girls had many diverse relationships with multiple texts and literacy practices. However, these literacy practices did not translate into success in the classroom. My study indicated that inequalities based on class and race were still a key driving force in the girls' relationships with schools and learning. George Counts wrote in 1932, "On all genuinely crucial matters the school follows the wishes of the groups or classes that rule society" (p. 25). Unfortunately, this is still true today. Although Lincoln Middle School had a diverse student body and claimed to support all students, in subtle and not-so-subtle ways, the school still privileged students who were White and middle class. In addition, based on economic privileges, some students had more resources and encouragement to support them in their learning at school as well as for planning for their academic and vocational futures. The girls with the most economic resources were the most academically successful in school and the most articulate about plans for their futures. On the other hand, Erika, the poorest and most marginalized student in my study, barely passed 8th grade; when asked where she saw herself in ten years, one of her answers was "in bed, asleep."

Throughout the time I spent with these students, I also discovered time and spaces where the girls used their voices, were active agents in their learning, and found allies within the school system who supported authentic academic and personal growth. When the girls were given opportunities to engage with texts that were relevant to them, even the student who spent most of her time in class silent with her head on her desk came alive. However, many of the topics that were most engaging and significant to the girls—the media, sexuality, teen pregnancy, violence, and race—were deemed inappropriate by the school system. Their academic experiences were punctuated by silences of the school classroom culture. As Moniqua describes in the earlier poem, their inner selves, which are "full of colors and full of personality," didn't have much space within the middle school classroom.

Chapter 1 focuses on Lincoln Middle School as the research site. It describes the Girls Literacy Discussion Group and my role in the group.

Chapter 2 provides a theoretical framework for work on girls and literacies.

Chapter 3 illustrates how the girls used their bodies as texts to perform identities. For example, though she was born in Iran, Moniqua performed as a "Spanish" or "Hispanic" student to fit in with the dominant race of her social group. Erika was a low-income student who performed a middle-class identity in the Girls Literacy Discussion Group. Tetra was a White lesbian/bisexual student who performed a "geek" identity in order to resist compulsory femininity as well as maintain her class and race privilege.

In Chapter 4, I describe the role of mass media in the girls' lives and their multiple responses to these texts. When responding to texts such as teen magazines, music videos, commercials, and movies, sometimes the girls were passive recipients of corporate messages and at other times they were critical thinkers. This chapter speaks to the need for critical feminist media literacy skills in middle school classrooms.

Chapter 5 highlights the girls' interest in texts that explore sexualities. This chapter points to the need of adolescent girls for authentic dialogue about bodies and sexualities.

In Chapter 6, violence is investigated as a text in girls' lives, using Erika as an example. Erika lived with both domestic violence and neighborhood gang violence. Classrooms can be more inclusive spaces for disengaged students like Erika when there is room for their lived realities.

Chapter 7 examines how the girls used the Internet, creative writing, and drawing to build resiliency and a sense of agency. For example, Tetra, as a young lesbian/bisexual, used the Internet to connect with a larger queer community that she did not have access to at her school. Kaliya, an African American student in a school with very few Black students, also used the Internet to access a larger African American community.

Chapter 8 investigates Erika as a silent, disengaged, and failing student. Through a documentation of the places, spaces, and times that Erika did speak and the topics she spoke about, a larger pattern emerged. Disengaged students like Erika are silent, not because they have nothing to say, but because their voices and experiences are deemed "unacceptable" in the public middle school setting. Teachers must take the risk of using a multiple literacies framework to see students' complete literacy practices as well as create spaces for all students' voices.

Chapter 9 focuses on girls and the achievement gap, with Tetra and Erika as two examples of how social capital affects school achievement, future planning, and narratives of the future. The book concludes with a resounding appeal for educators to rise to the challenge of embracing a commitment to a multiple literacies framework in order to promote social justice in our schools.

> "I want to read my life in a book," Moniqua said one day in the Girls
>   Literacy Discussion Group.
> Not missing a beat, her friend Kaliya answered, "That would be a
>   dangerous book." Both girls laughed.

This book offers significant implications and concrete examples for educators, parents, administrators, and policy makers on how to improve educational practices for marginalized students such as the girls in this study. The implications of this research are concrete solutions for middle school teachers who want to improve the literacy development of students in their classroom. This book is an important update to the understandings of how adolescents use texts to form complex, hybrid, and multifaceted identities that include the intertwining of race, class, gender, and sexual identity. This book is, in fact, "dangerous," as Kaliya pointed out, in its deviance from simple and linear understandings of both literacy and girls' lives; instead, it interrupts the dominant narratives of adolescent girls to provide a space for the voices of these marginalized students to come alive.

CHAPTER 1

Lincoln Middle School and the Girls Literacy Discussion Group

When the bell rings at Lincoln Middle School, the hallways swell with students laughing, pushing each other, talking loudly, and grabbing books from their lockers. As passing period ends, the commotion dies down, leaving trails of candy wrappers, lost papers, and a few students lingering in the corridor. It probably looks like any other day at thousands of middle schools across the country.

LINCOLN MIDDLE SCHOOL

Lincoln Middle School is a large public middle school in a city in the southwest United States. It is an urban public school in one of the largest school districts in the country. In this school district, students have about a 50% chance of graduating from high school with their peers. The rates are worse for students of color; Hispanic students had an additional 18% chance of not graduating compared to their White peers; for Native American students, it was almost an additional 25% chance.

Lincoln Middle School has interesting demographics for an urban public school. Whereas the student body in most schools in this district are either overwhelmingly White or almost completely Hispanic, Lincoln Middle School is one of a handful that is more evenly divided. Of its 900 students, 51% identified as Anglo, 34% as Hispanic, 6% as Native American, 5% as African American, 2% as Asian, and 2% as other ethnicity (terms used in school district data). In most schools in the district, either many (over 50%) or few (10% or less) students receive free lunches. In contrast, 34% of the students at Lincoln Middle School receive free lunches.

This unique diversity is due, in part, to the fact that Lincoln Middle School is on the periphery of a neighborhood sometimes referred to as the "Whites" due to its concentration of White residents compared to the rest of the city. The school is bordered on two sides by two main city avenues. On these sides of the school there are many apartment buildings and housing developments. On the other two sides of the school, beyond the soccer field and portable buildings, is a quieter, more suburban-looking neighborhood dominated by single-family homes. Lincoln Middle School feeds into two different high schools: one squarely in the "Whites," with more White and relatively higher-income students, and the other, closer to downtown, with more students of color and low-income students. Lincoln Middle School is a place where these diverse student populations overlap more than they did in elementary school or will in high school.

Despite this diversity, the teaching staff at Lincoln Middle School is predominantly White women, while nearly all of the support staff (janitorial, cafeteria, educational assistants, and secretaries) are people of color, mostly Hispanic. Nearly 50 out of 55 of the regular education teachers and all of the administrators are White. These demographics mirror public school teachers across the United States, where 84% of U.S. public school teachers are women and 84% are White (Feistritzer, Griffin, & Linnajarvi, 2011). The school is rated as not meeting Adequate Yearly Progress (AYP) as determined by No Child Left Behind (NCLB) in reading. Only 54.5% of all students tested as reading proficient or above, and the rates were lower for Hispanic (50%), Native American (38%), and economically disadvantaged students (40%).

THE GIRLS LITERACY DISCUSSION GROUP

The main source of data collection for my research was an 18-week Girls Literacy Discussion Group, which met once a week for one 50-minute class period. The six participants, all 8th-grade girls, were drawn from the same language arts class. The participants were chosen by purposeful sampling for maximum variation and diversity in terms of race, ethnicity, class, and oral participation in class (see Table 1.1). The participants included both struggling and successful readers, as defined by the language arts teacher, in order to provide a greater richness and depth of data based on students' diverse experiences with literacy.

Definitions of Terms:

Race: The racial term or terms that the participants used to self-identify, except for Moniqua, which includes both self-identification and teacher identification.

Class: The terms are based on Gilbert-Kahl Model of the Class Structure in *The American Class Structure* (1998).

Table 1.1. Characteristics of Participants

Participant	Race	Class	Academic Achieve-ment	Voice	Family Information	Other Information
Angela	Half Hispanic, half White	Working class	C	Middle	Lived with sister at cousin's house.	Practicing Christian.
Chris	Navajo	Middle class	A	Quiet	Lived with both parents and sister.	Was formerly in gifted program.
Erika	Hispanic	Working poor	Failing	Quiet	Lived with mother and brother, parents divorced. Father in and out of prison and involved with local gangs.	New to school. Left past school for fighting and failing grades. Commutes from across town. Formerly in special education.
Kaliya	African American	Middle class	B	Loud	Parents divorced and lived in two houses.	Computer savvy.
Moniqua	Self-identified as "Hispanic." Teacher identified as "Other."	Middle class	B	Loud	Only child living with single mother. Mother is a nurse, often working night shifts.	Outspoken, most vocal member of Girls Literacy Discussion Group.
Tetra	White	Upper middle class	A	Middle	Lives with sister and both parents	Self-identified as "lesbian," "bisexual," "butch," and "tomboy."

Academic Achievement: Their spring mid-term language arts grade.

Family Information: Synthesized from individual and group interviews.

Voice: The concept of voice emerges from both feminist research and research on marginalized students exploring the silencing that occurs in schools (Fine, 1991; Fine & Weis, 2003; Fordham, 1997). Voice is framed as the opposite of silence and refers to taking up space in the classroom. In Signithia Fordham's essay "Those Loud Black Girls," she builds upon Grace Evans's (1997) language to paint a picture of Black girls who refuse to be "voiceless or silent," refuse to be "seen rather than heard, to be passive rather than assertive" (Fordham, 1997, p. 97), which in her study she found to be requisite for African American girls to be successful in school. The concept of voice, loudness, and marginalization in school continues to be a salient issue. Here "voice" refers to how often the girls spoke out loud (not including whispering to a classmate) during teacher-led language arts classroom activities, as recorded on three occasions and averaged. "Loud" means they spoke several times during the class period, "middle" means speaking once or twice, and "quiet" means not speaking at all.

The focus of the Girls Literacy Discussion Group was on the texts the girls encountered in their lives and how they used these texts and their multiple literacies to make sense of the world around them as well as themselves in their worlds. My definition of text was a broad one. Following in the tradition of other researchers who have examined multiple literacies, I looked at text as "an ordered set of signs from which one constructs meaning" (Huot, Stroble, & Bazerman, 2004, p. 279). These texts are "free from a specific site or set of practices" (Huot, Stroble, & Bazerman, 2004, p. 4). Therefore, in addition to written words, music, art, visual expression, craft, and voice were all considered texts with which girls interact.

Our meeting time was first thing in the morning. The girls would go to their language arts class for attendance, and I would come to pick them up. While the girls were preparing to come with me, other students in the class were beginning to take out their books for silent reading. Every so often a particular boy in the class would say to me, "Take me! I can be a girl!"

The girls always seemed excited to come to the Girls Literacy Discussion Group, or at least to get out of silent reading in the language arts class. We would walk down the hallway together, the girls talking with each other or with me, in groups of two or three, sometimes stopping to greet a friend. On several occasions I overheard one of them saying, "Yeah, I'm going to my girls group," with a tinge of pride in her voice. They seemed to feel special to be part of the Girls Literacy Discussion Group.

I chose to use a discussion group because it is particularly suited to adolescent girls (Carico, 2001; Haiken, 2002; Weis & Carbonell-Medina, 2003). Studies have indicated that in a research situation where there is an inherent imbalance of power between an adult researcher and youth participants, group discussions can allow for a safer and more comfortable environment for the participants by allowing them to be with their peers, to have more room to lead group discussions, and to receive validation from others in the group. "It is believed that the group situation may reduce the influence of the interviewer on the research subjects by tilting the balance of power towards the group" (Madriz, 2000, p. 838). Especially for adolescent girls, the issue of feeling safe enough to express their ideas may be mediated by the group discussion. "Because focus groups emphasize the collective, rather than the individual, they foster free expression of ideas, encouraging the members of the group to speak up," (p. 838). Madriz also notes that group discussions may be particularly useful to girls of color. Focus groups "represent a methodology that is consistent with the particularities and everyday experiences of women of color. Women have historically used conversation with other women as a way to deal with their oppression," (p. 839).

I chose which girls to invite into the group and then they decided whether or not to participate, with parental permission. I observed the class before selecting my ideal participants based on purposeful sampling coupled with diversity according to my criteria. Then I held a meeting for those girls I had selected where I went over what the group would look like and what we'd be doing. All but one selected participant chose to be in the group.

My role in the group was a complex one. I came to the group as a researcher and group facilitator, rather than a teacher. However, the role I played with them was more similar to "teacher" than anything else they had experienced in the school setting. In addition, because I had taught at the school a few years prior to the study, my relationship with the school faculty placed me as a "teacher." I tried to interrupt this framing; I did not want to be seen as the girls' "teacher." After all, I was not grading the girls or reporting anything back to the language arts teacher; yet this unspoken role of "teacher" was hard to shake in this institutional setting. For example, following the rules of the school, I was required to escort the girls from their classroom to our meeting space in another classroom, rather than allow them to walk by themselves, which I would have preferred. When two girls left the Girls Literacy Discussion Group one day to go to the bathroom, they were chastised by a teacher in the hall and told they had to have their teacher (me) give them a hall pass first. I told the girls that since I was not a teacher there, they could call me by my first name, Hadar, as opposed to the more formal "Ms." or "Mrs." titles used by teachers at the school. However, several times some of the girls called me "Ms. Hadar," indicating that I inhabited a space in their minds, perhaps not exactly equivalent, but similar to, a teacher. Whether I was seen as a "teacher" or some other ambiguous benevolent adult within the school, I was clearly an adult while they were adolescents, a relationship that, in our society and in schools in particular, automatically establishes a power imbalance.

My goal as a researcher was to decrease the potential centrality of my own voice as the one adult in the group and instead highlight their words, experiences, and dialogue. I used several techniques to help with this process, the first being active and respectful listening as delineated by Oliver and Lalik (2000). Active and respectful listening includes not only removing my voice from the center of the discussion but also "putting aside evaluation or judgment of the worthiness of the knowledge that the girls were sharing" (Oliver & Lalik, 2000, p. 324). Such listening allowed the girls to set the tone and direction of the conversation, even if it wasn't apparently "useful" to my research. For example, one day the girls spent nearly 20 minutes discussing what to do if a friend had bad breath; it was a conversation that tired me but was significant to them.

The act of listening was coupled with strategic questioning, which Oliver and Lalik (2000) refer to as "not the formal critical questions found in the literature on critical literacy but rather small questions such as 'What do you mean by that?'" (p. 325). These questions "help the girls extend and analyze their language and become more aware of conditions that influence the way they are learning to think about [themselves]" (p. 325). By extending their dialogue with questions, again, my own voice and opinions were de-centered while they expressed their viewpoints, opinions, and processes.

Like Bettie (2003) in her study of adolescent girls, "I never lied about my age, extent of education, or other facts about my life, but didn't disclose much unless asked" (p. 20). I did mention basic facts about myself: that I had lived in New York City, that I was Jewish, that I went to college, that I had a son, and that I took dance classes. But I didn't directly discuss my family configuration, sexual orientation, racial identification, or class background. Although I'm sure that based on my appearance, dress, mannerisms, and way of speaking, the girls came to certain conclusions about who I was in the world. The girls' perceptions of me seemed to vary depending on who they were. Again, I wanted to center their experiences, and they became the focus of the conversations, though I was certainly an integral part of the group and the group experience.

In addition to the Girls Literacy Discussion Group meetings, I also conducted individual interviews with participants and teachers over the course of the entire school year. I recorded many hours of observations of the students in their classes, the lunchroom, hallways, and outside areas. I collected artifacts from the school, the classrooms, and the girls themselves in order to better understand their diverse literacy practices. Some of the school and out-of-school work they shared with me included language arts writing folders, individual portfolios, essays they wrote, notes they wrote to their friends, e-mails, and websites downloaded from the Internet. The students also created several pieces of writing and artwork during the Girls Literacy Discussion Group. These pieces were responses to questions posed that directly fed into an understanding of the overall research question. For example, students were given questionnaires about their reading and writing habits, asked to list their favorite books, given paper to draw their homes and literacy activities within them. They were asked to draw a Venn diagram about themselves in 6th and 8th grade and to complete a small booklet, with sentence starters, about themselves. The purpose of this work was to give the students another way, besides the interview process, to examine the issues of their own literacy development and identity construction.

My data analysis was rooted in a model of constructivist grounded theory (Charmaz 2006; Creswell, 2007). As a grounded theorist, I used simultaneous collection of data and analysis, coding, comparative methods, memo writing, and theoretical sampling to integrate the data to construct a grounded theory (Charmaz, 2006). The creation of a rich, deep understanding requires "careful, systematic and detailed description through watching, listening to and interacting with the actors over a sustained period of time, the tracing and interpretation of emergent themes and the piecing together these themes into an aesthetic whole" (Lawrence-Lightfoot & Davis, 1997, p. 12). As a qualitative study, the issue of the trustworthiness of the study is central. The trustworthiness of this study is secured by its use of prolonged engagement, triangulation, member checking, use of the researcher's journal, and peer debriefing.

I triangulated my data by using multiple methods of data collection (Creswell, 2007), including observations, the discussion group, individual interviews, and the collection of artifacts. In addition, data came from several sources, including the school, the classroom, the teacher, the six participants, and three key informants. The process of triangulation occurred during data collection as a core element of data analysis, as is usual in grounded theory research. By constant comparison across multiple sources and methods, "each data source provides corroborative evidence to verify information obtained by other methods," resulting in "a holistic understanding of the situation and generally converging conclusions" (Anafara, Brown, & Mangione, 2002, p. 33).

I chose to write in an accessible format about the students in the Girls Literacy Discussion Group because I wanted to "move beyond the academy's inner circle" and speak in a language that can reach teachers, parents, and other educators: those of us who are in the trenches working directly with young people as well as those who make decisions that influence their lives (Lawrence-Lightfoot & Davis, 1997, p. 10). I was moved by the questions posed by Laurel Richardson (1992): "How do we create texts that are vital? That are attended to? That make a difference?" (p. 923). My goal is for this book to make a difference in the real lives of real middle school girls.

CHAPTER 2

Understanding Girls and Literacies

In the Girls Literacy Discussion Group, I used a multiple literacies framework to investigate their sites, modes, and forms of literacy practices. While early concepts of literacy limited the definition of literacy to just reading and writing, current literacy theory recognizes the need to include multiple texts and ways of knowing in order to understand the complex and dialectic nature of literacy (Alvermann et al., 2006; Hagood, 2009; Huot, Stroble, & Bazerman, 2004; Knobel & Lankshear, 2007). A new literacies perspective "posits that literacy is no longer singular and print bound; instead the iconic and digital demands of the 21st century have opened up literacies that transverse across print and nonprint based formats" (Skinner & Licktenstein, 2009, p. 91). A text is understood as "anything that can be read and comprehended or constructed to share meaning and includes reading, writing/designing, speaking, listening and viewing," (p. 91). For the girls in this book, texts such as music videos, movies, teen magazines, e-mail, conversations over the Internet, and creative writing were central in their literacy practices.

MULTIPLE LITERACIES

In addition to including multiple texts, multiple literacies also encompass "many ways of constructing, reading, knowing, and reproducing texts" (Obidah, 1998, p. 52). There are many ways of understanding the world and, therefore, multiple approaches to texts. Likewise, Gee (1989) states, "Literacy is always plural: literacies—there are many of them since there are many secondary Discourses, and we all have some and fail to have others" (p. 9). Building on the work of the New London Group Cope and Kalantzis (2000) constructed a framework for multiple literacies, or what they called "multilateralism," which has three major components: use of multimodality (integration of more than one design in one text), intertextuality (examination of relationships and references between and among texts), and hybridity (creation of new meanings and genre by the interaction of texts).

Current understandings have added "new literacies" to the defini-tion of multiple literacies (Hagood, 2009; Knobel & Lankshear, 2007). These new literacies include not only technology itself but also the "par-ticipation, collaboration, dispersion and distributed expertise of literacy practices" (Hagood, 2009, p. 1). These new literacy practices and forms are multimodal, hybrid, evolving, and shifting rapidly (Alvermann, 2009; Hagood, 2009; Knobel & Lankshear, 2007). Multiple literacies, including new literacies, have been in the forefront of current understandings of youth literacies and, particularly important here, middle school literacies.

Students use literacy as a way to make meaning through interaction with a text. Rosenblatt (1994) developed the idea that literacy is meaning-making, or a transaction between the reader and the text. According to Rosenblatt's transactional theory of reading and writing, a reader interacts with a text, bringing to it his or her particular way of understanding the world through past experiences and present understandings. This trans-action between the text and the reader results in meaning-making. "The 'meaning' does not reside ready-made 'in' the text or 'in' the reader but happens or comes into being during the transaction between reading and text" (Rosenblatt, 1994, p. 24). Rosenblatt also names the context in which an individual brings to a text his or her "linguistic-experiential reservoir" (p. 42). This reservoir includes cultural, social, and personal history and past experiences with language.

In this way, literacy is "a dynamic process, involving interaction and transaction between people, texts, and contexts" (Moje, Dillon, & O'Brian, 2000, p. 165). We can see that literacy is social and therefore is relational and transactional by nature. Students do not "achieve" lit-eracy as if it is a checklist of benchmarks that one has attained; they use literacies to make meaning in their lives. "Literacy is not a set of neutral skills that can be transferred to any task once mastered. Literacy medi-ates social relationships and ideological values" (Dyson, 1999, p. 157). Therefore, "the meanings people make of texts and of literacy events are contextualized by the social networks or communities and historical and cultural arrangements in which persons live, work, and play" (Moje et al., 2000, p. 167). Literacy serves to strengthen social and relational con-nections between girls and larger communities that represent particular aspects of themselves and who they are becoming in the world.

Literacy is rooted not only in a social context but also in a cultural and ideological context. Gee (1989) defines literacy as "mastery of or fluent con-trol over a secondary Discourse" (p. 6), with *Discourse* defined as ways of being in the world or "the forms of life with which we integrate words, acts, values, beliefs, attitudes and social identities . . . a sort of 'identity kit' which comes complete with the appropriate costume and instructions on how to act, talk and often write" (pp. 6–7). This definition is useful in that it places literacy practices within a particular cultural and ideological context. Researchers have documented the ways that literacy events and literacy acts are situated in specific cultural, historical, and institutional contexts (Gee, 2000; Heath, 1984 Scribner & Cole, 1981; Street, 1984). "The meanings people make of texts and of literacy events are contextualized by the social networks or communities and historical and cultural arrangements in which persons live, work, and play" (Moje, et al., 2000, p. 167). Therefore, literacy must be understood as both transactional and bound by particular contexts.

The girls in my study used literacy practices to affirm identities, gain exposure to new positions, build community, and connect with others. I am using the term *literacy practices* to signify a broad range of ways to use language, including engagement with reading, writing, discourse, music, creative text, and critical perspectives. This definition is supported by Alvermann (2004), who urges educators to broaden the term of literacies "to include the performative, visual, aural and semiotic understandings necessary for constructing and reconstructing print and non-print-based texts" (p. viii). This includes voice, silence, and narrative as literacy practices as well as the use of the body as a text to convey meaning.

The body can be seen as a text which the girls used in the construction and communication of their identity performances. As Rebecca Walker (2003) writes: "In our North American culture, and indeed in cultures around the world, the body is a sign, a text to be read and interpreted," (p. xv). By the body, theorists mean not only the physical body in terms of size and form but also adornment of the body, such as fashion and hairstyle, as well as the body as a sexual agent and sexual object. These embodiments, such as dress, stance, and pose, are all "cultural symbols manipulated to express the self" (Bloustein, 2003, p. 70). Therefore, one can read the body as one reads other symbols. The appropriation of particular body symbols signifies distinction from others as well as belonging, thus communicating cultural norms, resistance, and a sense of self. For middle school girls, the body becomes a text to communicate constructed identity. "Girls' rhetoric of self-making were enacted through their bodies, their explorations involving negotiation of both similarity and difference, the marking of boundaries between self and other" (Bloustein, 2003, p. 68). For the middle school girls in my study, the body was a significant text to read in order to understand their processes of meaning-making and constructions of self.

CRITICAL LITERACY

The need for development of critical literacy emerged as a key implication for educators. Critical literacy places literacy within a theoretical framework that acknowledges not only the relational and social context of literacy but also one that is attuned to the imbalances of the power in-fluencing literacy development and construction. "Critical literacy refers to an awareness that the language of texts and the reader's responses to it are not neutral but are shaped by social contexts and our experiences as people of particular races, ethnicities, genders, and social classes" (Young, 2001, p. 5). Furthermore, critical literacy includes examination of how texts can either reinforce hegemonic ideas of power and privilege, or work to create transformation in the world, or both. The girls at Lincoln Middle School demonstrated emergent critical literacy skills and perspectives.

For Freire and Macedo (1987), literacy is "fundamental to aggressive-ly constructing one's voice as part of a wider project of possibility and empowerment" (p. 7). To be literate is to read the world, that is, to be able to name ones experience and critically situate oneself in the world. "For the notion of literacy to become meaningful," writes Freire in Freire and Macedo (1987), "it has to be situated within a theory of cultural produc-tion and viewed as an integral part of the way in which people produce, transform and reproduce meaning" (p. 142). Reading the world is central to being able to read the word, and both can be used as praxis, that is, "reflection and action upon the world in order to change it" (Freire, 1993, p. 33). In this sense, Freire's view of literacy is very close to bell hooks's (1989) notion of "coming to voice" (p. 54). Both theorists speak to the need for individuals to use texts to form a critical consciousness about them-selves and their worlds.

The use of critical literacy is crucial to the examination of multiple lit-eracies and their interaction with adolescents. Critical literacy compels the reader to engage in disrupting the commonplace, interrogating multiple viewpoints, focusing on sociopolitical issues, and taking action to pro-mote social justice (Lewison, Flint, & Van Sluys, 2002). Training in critical analysis is crucial for adolescents so that they can deconstruct the mul-tiple and often contradictory messages they receive from their interactions with multiple texts. "A necessary component of reconceptualizing adoles-cent literacy and of literacy success in the 21st century, critical literacy is a means for analyzing how powerful institutional contexts (such as formal schooling) act as regulating institutions for knowledge and resources" (Hagood, 2002, p. 248). Attention also needs to be given to developing a critical approach to media texts and literacies. In a complex world of intertexuality, hybridity, and multimodalities, the need for adolescents' to identify, question, and problematize the realities presented and produced by texts is even more evident:

> Given the dangerous and problematic nature of literacies to produce selective
> views of the world, critical literacy has been deemed an important and

needed aspect of literacy instruction for supporting and interrogating young people's knowledge of how the texts they use—such as grunge rock, fashion magazine, or news accounts—figure into their understandings of themselves and of their everyday lives. (Hagood, 2002, p. 247)

Issues of voice and silence are crucial when examining critical perspective on literacy. Low-income students, students of color, girls, and other marginalized students are particularly at risk of being ignored, dismissed, and otherwise silenced in schools. Several researchers have found that the giving priority to finding one's voice, discussing various perspectives, and developing critical thinking are much more prevalent in classrooms with upper- and middle-class students than in those with predominantly working-class students (Anyon, 1997; Finn, 2009; Weis, 1990). Furthermore, researchers have explored how voice and silence play a role in the lives of girls in particular (Barbieri, 1995; Fordham, 1997; Hall, 2011). Understanding how silence and voice interplay with students' multiple literacy practices is essential in conceptualizing marginalized students' literacies.

UNDERSTANDING GIRLS AND ADOLESCENCE

Finders (1997), in *Just Girls: Hidden Literacies and Life in Junior High,* urges educators and researchers to dismiss the three key myths of adolescence: that there is a universal experience of adolescence, that adolescence is a negative period, and that adolescents seek to sever ties with adults. Instead, she and other theorists argue that we need to see adolescents as situated in diverse sociocultural contexts that frame adolescence (Alvermann, 2009; Hall, 2011; Lesko, 2001). Researchers, educators, and parents are urged to stop assuming that young people are struggling with problems any more or less than are children or adults (Moje, 2002), recognize that adolescent culture is not in opposition to adult culture or marked by alienation from adults, and realize that there are genuine connections between adults and youth (Collins, 2009).

In U.S. society, adolescence has generally been construed as the period between childhood and adulthood. Traditional structuralist perspectives of adolescence often essentialize adolescence as a period of "storm and stress" (Finders, 1997). In popular culture, adolescents are typically either demonized or trivialized as dangerous, lazy, unpredictable, defiant, and irresponsible (Finders, 1997; Lesko, 2001; Moje, 2002). These stereotypes cross with race, class, and gender, resulting in such images as the White, rich, clueless girl; the dangerous gangster boy of color; and the poor, Black, irresponsible teen mother (Giroux, 1998). Such narratives reflect the biases and power structures of the larger hegemonic society. "Any discourse about youth is simultaneously a narrative about the ideologies and social practices that structure adult society" (Giroux, 1998, p. 3). Any study of what it means to be a girl must simultaneously deconstruct cultural and examine societal definitions of girlhood.

Theories on adolescence can be broken down into two main trajectories, the first being more traditional, evolving from the field of psychology, and the second, more recent, growing out of cultural studies. The traditional perspectives of adolescence are rooted in psychological grand theories of human development. According to these theories, adolescence is a time for identity versus role confusion (Erikson, 1968), achievement of a masculine or feminine role (Havigvurst & Taba, 1949), leaps in cognitive development (Elkind, 1981), and biological transformations (Newman & Newman, 1986). Feminists in the field of psychology have critiqued this literature for relying on a male lens rather than looking at the specific experiences of girls (Brown & Gilligan, 1992; Chodorow, 1978; Gilligan, Lyons, & Hanmer, 1990). Postmodern critiques of these bodies of literature reject the notion of adolescence, for either boys or girls, as a fixed state of life ruled by biological forces of puberty and cognitive development and instead see the concepts of "girlhood" and adolescence as socially constructed and shifting (Lesko, 2001; Walkerdine, Lucey, & Melody, 2001). Postmodern theorists argue that adolescence is not a universal biological condition that girls pass through uniformly and press for a re-examination of studies that essentialize adolescent girls or the concept of girlhood.

In this sense, a girl's identity is not rooted in a "stable, internal sense of being" (Lewis, Encisco, & Moje, 2007) but instead constructs a sense of self that is hybrid in nature, shifting, performative, and situated in time and space. Girls' identities are not fixed but fluid. For example, a girl who attends one middle school where she is "popular" may move to another school where her identity shifts to being an "outsider." Even race and class are situated identities; in one school or situation a student may be seen as "rich" and in another "poor." In this study, as described in Chapter 3, Monique shifts how she places herself racially to affiliate with a certain peer group. Rather than viewing adolescent identity formation as a series of prescribed checkpoints along a linear path, I, like others, see the middle school years as part of a complex journey with many diverse influences as identities stabilize and destabilize when the individual interacts with changes in discourses and social spaces.

Conceptualizing Gender, Race, and Class

When examining the literacy experiences of adolescents, we must include a critical analysis of how race, class, and gender play a role in the larger hegemonic society as well as in their day-to-day lives. Theorists and researchers have pointed to the need for theoretical perspectives on adolescents that integrate gender, race, and class analysis (Cammarota & Romero, 2006; Leadbeater & Way, 2007; Lopez, 2003; Weis & Fine, 2005). Finders (1997) notes that there are "multiple and competing influences that shape how one enters adolescence . . . despite outward signs of homogeneity, diversity shapes how one embarks on the journey toward adulthood. Adolescence, then, cannot be examined without regard to race, class, or gender" (p. 121). The findings of my study have been framed by a large body of research that incorporates analysis of gender, race, class, and sexuality, and how they influence the literacies and lives of adolescents.

According to a social constructivist perspective, gender is a social construction (Bornstein, 1994; Butler, 1999; Finders, 1997). In most cultures, one is assigned a gender at birth based on the presence or absence of a penis (Bornstein, 1994). Gender assignment may differ from gender identity, which is an internal sense of gendered self. Whereas an internal sense of gender may be fluid, society has created a rigid gender binary. Gender has been used by society to assign meanings to individuals and create a hierarchy of power and social status. Gender influences both how we are seen by society and how we see ourselves. Adolescents form their identities and sense of self within a gendered society and, therefore, are influenced by messages about gender and gender roles. Likewise, gender intersects with race and ethnicity to create racialized and gendered stereotypes such as the submissive Asian woman, the Jewish American princess, and the sexually aggressive Black woman (Brodkin, 1998; Fine & Weis, 2003; Hall, 2011; Hernandez & Rehman, 2002; Leadbeater & Way, 2007). For example, in this study the girls of color faced different stereotypes than the White girls at the school.

Young women, in their process to make meaning of themselves in the world, navigate society's shifting and hybrid gendered expectations. Performance theorists note that gender can be viewed as a performance with a constructed gendered identity that shifts based on the particular social context (Butler, 1999). Queer theorists, in particular, frame femininity as a gender performance (Fausto-Sterling, 2000 Halberstam, 1998; Payne, 2002). In adolescence there is increased pressure on girls for a feminized gender performance. In addition, constructions of femininity are influenced by race and class. For example, Bettie (2003), in her study of adolescent girls at a California school, found that "girls performed different versions of femininity that were integrally linked to and inseparable from their class and racial/ethnic performances" (p. 5). Likewise in this study, the girls constructed embodied gender performances based on class and racial communities and identities.

Race has been one of the "fundamental organizing principles of U.S. society" (Lopez, 2003, p. 17). Race is a social construction in that it has no biological basis; instead, its meanings are socially and historically constructed (Omi & Winant, 1994). While race is a social construction, it has tangible consequences in the real world. Whiteness is more than just a binary opposition to Blackness; it also carries social power and cultural capital. Groups and individuals are assigned racial meanings that result in economic, social, and political classification. Cultural and ethnic groups are racially assigned, and meanings are constructed based on these positionings.

Researchers have documented how U.S. public schools on the whole have privileged and continue to privilege White students over students of color (Bernal et al., 2006; Fordham, 1996; Fordham & Ogbu, 1986; Horsford, 2011; Valencia, 2011; Weis & Fine, 2005 Winn, 2011). This discrimination positions students of color and White students differently within the schooling context, influencing their own perceptions of self as students and their relationships to schools and literacy. Schools in the United States historically have been steeped in Whiteness, privileging White culture, language, and experiences. For students of color, there is a "legacy of denying equality in education and miseducation throughout America's history" (Winn, 2011, p. 111). This legacy leads not only to a perennial achievement gap between White students and students of color but also to a discipline gap, whereby "Black, Latino, and American Indian students encounter more discipline sanctions in school than their White counterparts," ultimately leading to a racialized school-to-prison pipeline for a disproportionate number of urban youth of color (Winn, 2011, p. 111). These inequalities continue today, as documented in my study.

Even public schools with diverse student populations, like Lincoln Middle School, find ways to reproduce racial and socioeconomic tracking within the school itself (Brantlinger, 2003; Kelly 2008; Lopez, 2003; Oakes, 2005, 2008). "School practices (re)produce racial and gender inequalities by using race, class, and gender as markers to track students within schools, even within de facto segregated schools" (Lopez, 2003, p. 56). At Lincoln Middle School one example of this tracking was the racialized gap in the percentage of White students versus students of color in the gifted program compared to the regular education and special education programs.

Racial analysis is complicated by intersections of race and gender (Bettie, 2003; Bucholtz, 2011; Collins, 2009; Evans-Winter, 2005; Hall, 2011; Hurtado, 2003; Lopez, 2003). Books like *Colonize This!* (Hernandez & Rehman, 2002), *Adios Barbie* (Edut, 1998), and *This Bridge We Call Home* (Anzaldúa & Keating, 2002) have emphasized the effects of both racism and colonialism on the educational history of girls of color. Particularly relevant to this study is the body of literature emerging from Chicana and Latina feminist scholars, which examines the intersections of race, class, and gender for Latina students (Bernal et al., 2006; Denner & Guzman, 2006; Hurtado, 2003; Torres, 2003). Many of these sources challenge deficit frameworks that have been used to explain Chicana/o educational inequalities and replace them with understandings of multiple layers of oppression and discrimination in U.S. public schools. This study contributes to the research that documents the hidden realities of students of color in a public school setting.

Racial identities are both imposed from the outside and self-constructed. Racial identity can be defined as a "sense of group or collective identity based on one's perception that he or she shares a common racial heritage with a particular racial group" (Helms, 1990, p. 3). Self-constructed racial identities are created within a context of outside racial assignment. Tatum (2003) notes that the aspects of our identities that are dissonant from those that are systematically advantaged by society are the ones that are the target of our own attention as well as that of others. it is our targeted identities that hold our attention and the dominant identities that often go unexamined" (p. 22). Self-constructed racial identities allow us to form collective identities and groupings that can promote social and political responses to oppression as well as personal and political empowerment (Collins, 2009). This study illustrates how several of the girls used racial identity as an integral piece of their sense of self, their sense of belonging in community, and their literacy practices.

Race, as a social construction, can also be seen as a performative act. These shifting performances play a role in adolescents' hybrid and multifaceted identity construction. The hybridity and multiplicity of racial identity can lead to contradiction and conflict as well as transformational consciousness. Young people, more than any other group, appear to represent the emergence of new forms of community, identity, and postmodern citizenship, "including more fluid understandings of family, community, race, and identity (Giroux, 1998, p. 6). In this study, Moniqua's approach to her racial identity is marked by a fluidity and performance that speaks to the complexity of girls' constructed senses of self.

In addition to gender and race, socioeconomic class shapes, privileges, and frames the lives, identities, and opportunities available to students.

Class is also informed by gender, racial, and ethnic variables and may at times be fluid rather than fixed. After all, "class is a relational identity and we must always contextualize it within communities because it is within the context of these communities that young people draw conclusions about themselves" (Bettie, 2003, p. 194). Like race, class can also be performative. A student can use class-based signifiers, such as dress, manner of speaking, mannerisms, or references, to indicate belonging in a certain class-based social group. In this sense, class is both a material location and a performed identity. For example, the girls in the study indicated that they chose certain hairstyles and outfits based on their social groupings, and the social groups were formed in part by race and class affiliations.

Many educational theorists have documented and explored how social class is reproduced, that is, how low-income students often—despite their values, desires, and even academic achievement—end up in low-income jobs. In many studies, schools are held accountable for reproducing the economic status quo (Anyon, 1997; Brantlinger, 2003; Counts, 1932; Fine, 1991; Hicks, 2002; Jones, 2006; Lareau, 2005; Weis, 2008; Weis & Fine, 2005; Willis, 1977). Bourdieu and Passeron (1977) explained the "inequalities in the academic attainment of children from the different social classes" as being a result of different linguistic and social capital; that is, students who are raised in upper- and middle-class families are given the social capital needed to succeed in school. Likewise, Bowles and Gintis (1976) asserted that schools are designed to reproduce the economic status quo, giving middle- and upper-class students more power and resources than working-class and low-income students. Fine's (1991) study of drop-outs found that institutional silencing, exclusion, and pushing out contribute to higher rates of leaving high school for low-income urban students of color. Fine (1991)noted that "in the United States, public schools, particularly secondary schools, were never designed for low-income students or students of color" (p. 31). Current research documents the unfortunate continuity of these inequities (Finn, 2009; Horsford, 2011; Oakes, 2008; Weis, 2008) Likewise, this study documents how students without social capital are at a disadvantage for achieving academically.

In addition, there are intersections between class and literacy. Socioeconomic class impacts the quality and flavor of literacy development (Finn, 2009; Heath, 1984; Hicks, 2002; Jones, 2006; Lareau, 2005). For example, Anyon's (1997) study of 5th-grade students found that curriculum, pedagogy, and approach to students' learning varied widely between schools with working-class, middle-class, and affluent students. Finn (1999, 2009), in his research on schools and working-class students, expands on this idea. He comments that in the United States "we have developed two kinds of education. First, there is empowering education, which leads to powerful literacy, the kind that leads to positions of power and authority. Second, there is domesticating education, which leads to functional literacy" (1999, p. ix). The first is given to students with class privilege and the second to poor and working-class students. Current trends continue these divisions: Students in high-poverty schools are more likely to be failing NCLB standards and therefore receiving packaged curriculum, while private schools and public schools with larger numbers of upper-class students are more likely to use creative teacher-developed lessons (Romero, 2007, p. 97).

The addition of a gendered analysis to the examination of class results in more multilayered understandings. Research on girls and class document how poverty and class privilege affect adolescent girls in unique ways (Bettie, 2003; Jones, 2006; Lutrell, 2003; Winn, 2011). For example, Jones (2006) examines the conversations of working-class girls about their mothers, a theme that arose in my study as well. Bettie (2003). notes that "common-sense class categories are infused with and intersect with gender and racial/ethnic meanings" (p. 7). As such, examinations of the intersections of gender, race, and class are critical in making meaning of the lived experiences of adolescent girls' lives, identities, and literacies.

Girls and Sexualities

Sexuality emerged as a significant theme for the girls at Lincoln Middle School. Much of the literature on youth and sexuality has focused on the negative consequences of sexual behavior (Lutrell, 2003; Tolman, 2005; Weis & Carbonell-Medina, 2003). For example, Tolman (2005) noted that the tendency in funded research—evidenced by the prevalence of studies on adolescent female sexual behavior, such as use of contraception, HIV transmission, and incidents of sexual assault—is to focus on the risks of sexuality, often "singling out girls as the receptacle of our concerns" (pp. 9–10). Researchers have noted the silence and censorship regarding positive aspects of adolescent girls' sexuality (Fine & Weis, 2003; Tolman, 2005; Wolf, 1997). "The honest facts about female sexual development in adolescence—especially the facts of girls' desire—have sustained a long history of active censorship" (Wolf, 1997, p. xix). Likewise, girls in this study discussed the lack of information presented to them about sexuality.

Michelle Fine (1992), in her work on adolescent girls and sexuality, called these missing texts "the missing discourse of desire." She found, as did Tolman (2005), that female adolescent sexuality is defined "only in terms of disease, victimization and morality" and marked by an "avoidance of girls' own feelings of sexual desire and pleasure" (Tolman, 2005, p. 14). Whereas boys are presented as sexual agents, girls are presented as sexual objects, and their own experiences as sexual agents are missing as texts. "While sexualized images of adolescent girls are omnipresent, their sexual feelings are rarely if ever portrayed" (Tolman, 2005, p. 8). In a text-saturated world, these sexual images are even more present.

Wolf (1997) noted that adolescence is a time when most girls in our society are physically reined in by parents in an effort to protect their daughters from sexual violence or sexual activities. "The young girl's lust for space comes at the same moment her culture tells her that her developing body puts her in danger whenever she roams 'too far'" (p. 29). Some researchers found that the control can be flavored by race, class, and culture. Not all control comes from the family. Bloustein (2003), Dodson (1999), and Wolf (1997) in their studies examined how the term *slut*, like the word *ho*, has been used exclusively for girls, by both peer groups and the media, as a term "adopted to label and curtail girls' behavior and movement" (Bloustien, 2004, p. 94). Girls today, like the ones at Lincoln Middle School, continue to be bullied and harassed by these same terms.

The control is often linked to issues of pregnancy, a topic that also dominates research on adolescent girls (Tolman, 2005). Literature on the topic of pregnancy links teen pregnancy and economic class (Bettie, 2003; Edin & Kefalas, 2005; Lutrell, 2003). Bettie (2003) noted that "White middle-class performers were more likely than other girls to have abortions if they became pregnant, as a way of ensuring the life stages that their parents had in mind for them" (p. 68). In this study, the girls engaged with this discourse around pregnancy and economic class and added various viewpoints on abortion to the dialogue.

Queer theory, gay-and-lesbian studies, and lesbian feminist theory have contributed to understandings of middle school girls' sexualities. For Tetra, one of the key participants in the study, coming out as a lesbian/bisexual was a central element of her constructed identity and sense of self. Sexual identity was coupled with issues of gender expression as she also identified as a "butch" or "tomboy." Halberstam's (1998) theories of female masculinity informed my understanding of Tetra's gendered performances as a young butch lesbian. Writings emerging from queer studies have documented the lived experiences of other lesbian and queer youth (Baker, 2002; Driver, 2007; Horvitz, 2011; Kosciw, Greytak, Diaz, & Bartkiewicz, 2010; Sears, 2005). Lesbian feminist writers such as Gloria Anzaldúa, Audre Lorde, Adrienne Rich, and Dorothy Allison have brought rich analysis of the lesbian experience in their classic texts as they examined not only sexuality but also the dynamics of race, class, and ethnicity (Allison, 1994; Anzaldúa & Keating, 2002; Lorde, 1984; Rich, 1979). These texts have contributed to an understanding of adolescent female sexualities as complex, multifaceted, and significant identity markers in the lives of adolescent girls.

MIDDLE SCHOOL GIRLS AND LITERACIES

There are many different ways to look at girls and literacies. Other studies have examined the books girls read (Blackford, 2004; Cherland, 1994; DeBlase, 2003), how girls' literacies differ from boys' (Millard, 1997), and girls and media texts (Duke & Kreshel 1998; Durham, 1999; Gilbert & Taylor, 1991; Mazzarella & Pecora, 1999). More recent studies have focused on girls and their digital literacies, such as Morrison's (2010) work on teenage girls and their avatars; Lewis and Fabo's (2005) study of adolescent girls using instant messaging; Chandler-Olcott and Mahar's (2003) examination of adolescent girls writing anime; Warburten's (2010) examination of adolescent girls and Harry Potter fan fiction; Mazzarella's (2010) collection *Girl Wide Web 2.0* (2010); and Davis's (2010) study of girls' blogs.

This book joins the field of studies on adolescent girls and their literacies, adolescent girls in school, and adolescent girls and issues of race, class, gender, and sexuality. I like to think of this book as a more recent and updated version of Finders's (1997) *Just Girls: Hidden Literacies and Life in Junior High.* Finders, a middle school teacher, took time off from classroom teaching to examine the "literate underlife" of adolescent girls (p. 1) by conducting a year-long ethnographic study in a junior high school. There she documented how the girls used literacy practices to form social groups, perform constructed identities, and mark boundaries of belonging and difference. Similar themes emerge in this book, which adds to the conversation by incorporating analysis of technology and mass media, queer theory, gender expression and multiple sexualities, deepening understandings of race and class, and pushing the boundaries of multiple literacies.

CHAPTER 3

Using Texts to Perform Race and Class Identities

In the cafeteria at Lincoln Middle School, as in almost any other public middle school in the United States, students follow an invisible code. Although the members of the Girls Literacy Discussion Group may have enjoyed their conversations together during class time, taken risks in arguing controversial positions, or even shared intimate details about their lives, as soon as they walked down the hallway toward the cafeteria, they began to move away from one another. Tetra went to join the "Band Geeks," an almost completely White group of students who say they "enjoy school." Moniqua, Kaliya, and Erika found their social groups, all students of color and a mixture of boys and girls. Chris headed toward the other girls who play on the girls' basketball team, a mixed-race grouping. Angela searched for her one best friend, as they always had lunch together.

BODY AS TEXT

The social groupings were marked not only by interests but also by race and class identifications. Kaliya, Moniqua, and Erika were explicit in explaining that White students would not be welcome in their group of friends. Tetra was aware that her social group was almost all White. Class background was a more subtle divider but still discernible by interests, use of language, styles of clothing, and use of after-school time. These divisions are part of the hidden curriculum that all students must "read" and navigate as they make their way through middle school.

Race and class in the middle school context can be seen as performative acts. "Race and class were not merely nouns we used to narrate ourselves: they were verbs that governed how we interacted and performed in the midst of 'others'" (Giroux, 1998, p. 7). Students use racial and gendered performances to place themselves as insiders and outsiders vis-à-vis particular groupings and communities (Butler, 1999). Markers such as choice of music, hairstyle, language accents, and dress indicate race, class, and gender identity performances. These performances constitute a form of literacy as students use their bodies as texts to communicate belonging and identification. Moniqua, Erika, and Tetra provide three examples of how middle school girls use this body text to perform race and class identities in a diverse public school setting.

An Elusive Race Performance

The first time that Moniqua alluded to her own racial identity was during the third session of the Girls Literacy Discussion Group. The girls were talking about different cliques in school and where they each fit in. Kaliya turned to Moniqua: "Our group is mostly Spanish people, huh?"

"Mmm-hmm," replied Moniqua.

The question intrigued me since, from what the teachers had told me, neither Kaliya nor Moniqua was Hispanic according to official school categories, or Chicana, or "Spanish," as Kaliya described. I was told by Ms. Carpenter, their language arts teacher, that Kaliya was African American and that Moniqua had moved here from Iran; both of her parents were of Persian heritage, and she spoke Farsi (also known as Persian) at home.

"So what were you saying, your group is mostly . . ." I left the line
     lingering, waiting for one of them to fill it in.

"Hispanic," answered Moniqua.

"So why do you think that is?" I inquired.

"I don't know, that's just the way it is," Moniqua replied.

"If there were White kids who wanted to be in your group, do you
     think that would work?"

Moniqua laughed. "No, no."

At Lincoln Middle School, many of the social groups were split by race. In the Girls Literacy Discussion Group, only Chris, who identified as Navajo, and Angela, who called herself "half White and half Hispanic," said that their friends were both White and students of color. Tetra, who identified as White, stated that most of her friends were White, and Moniqua, Kaliya, and Erika were all part of the group mentioned above, which was mostly "Hispanic" or "Spanish."

When the Girls Literacy Discussion Group met the following week, Moniqua, while talking to Erika, directly identified herself as "Hispanic." On that day in the Girls Literacy Discussion Group, the girls played an ice-breaker game to give them a chance to get to know one another a little better. For this activity, the girls were divided into pairs. They were given a list of questions to ask each other. At the end, they reported back to the group what they had learned about their partner. Erika and

Moniqua were partners. When they returned to the group, here is what Erika said about Moniqua:

> Her name is Moniqua. She lives with her mom. She's 13 years old, little girl. She was born in Persia, right? She hangs out with Valerie; she talks on the phone and goes shopping. She's Christian. She's Hispanic. Her favorite movie is *Rose Red*. Her favorite TV show is *Friends*. The music she likes best is hip-hop. She has a cat. Her nickname is Moogles. She has no boyfriend but a friend. And what's unique about her is she doesn't get along with her mother; no sisters or brothers; she likes a lot of guys and she likes Pepsi.

Moniqua's dark hair and olive skin categorized her as a girl of color, a label she used to self-identify. However, like many girls of color in the United States, to the outside eye, her race was ambiguous, and malleable. As Mira Jacob (2003) wrote about growing up East Asian in the United States, "I was born with a mysterious face. My deep brown eyes and skin, the thick line of my black eyebrows and the slant of my cheekbones have always been described to me as exotic, haunting, elusive" (p. 4).

In our society, our bodies are texts that are read for racial identification, racial placement, and racial categorization. Race itself is a social construction with no biological basis; instead, it contains meanings that are socially and historically constructed (Omi & Winant, 1994). Based on the body as a text, individuals are assigned racial meanings that result in social, economic, and political classification. This categorization can vary from time to time and place to place. "I am shocked by the contextuality of identity," wrote Alsultany in *This Bridge We Call Home*. "That my body is marked as *gringa* in Costa Rica, as Latina in some U.S. contexts, Arab in others and some times and spaces not adequately Arab or Latina or 'American' and in other contexts simply as *other*" (Anzaldua & Keating, 2002, p. 107). These shifting performances play a role in the hybrid and multifaceted nature of identity construction.

Moniqua took the elusive qualities of her outer appearance and used them to pass as Chicana or "Hispanic," as she called it, the largest racial group at her middle school. She created a text or a narrative about her life and her identity that represented her sense of self in the world. As Jill Corral (2004), a daughter of Cuban immigrants raised in the Midwest, wrote, "Context is everything. I adopt the dress of different territories and travel through them to see if and where I could live in them. In the end though, it's usually a nice visit and a 'thanks I'm just *passing* through,'" (p. 120). The text Moniqua created was impermanent, experimental, and performative.

Moniqua's racial positioning reminded me of some of the writings of third-wave feminists who embrace inclusive, hybrid, and sometimes contradictory understandings of race and identity. As Ophira Edut (2003) wrote in her introduction to *Body Outlaws: Rewriting the Rules of Beauty and Body Image:*

> Rather than simply shun the idea of being defined by our appearances, young women today include our bodies as part of our multilayered self-definitions. In a world that still tries to assume our identities, we rebel with an outward expression of self. Our passion for the truth, in all its messy complexity, compels us to visibly defy easy categories and sweeping labels, even if they were created from within. . . .. Everything is up for questioning today—the media, our identities, each other. (p. xxii)

I, too, with my olive skin that turns dark brown in the summer, brownish-black curly/frizzy hair, and chocolate eyes have been misidentified as "Indian," "Hispanic," "part Black," and "mixed-race," though as a Jew with roots in Eastern Europe I identify as "White." I, too, was raised in public education settings where I was a minority; I didn't see girls who were brown and Jewish like me reflected back in the media or with teachers or other adults in the larger culture. I imagine it must be difficult for Moniqua as a young Persian/Iranian American young woman to work on forming her racial identity in a place where she sees no representations of herself, except possibly for negative stereotypes of Iranians and Iranian women. Even on government and school forms, Moniqua must search to find herself. In the U.S. Census, the only choices for racial identity for Iranian Americans are either "Other Asian" or "Some other race." One researcher found that "the confusion between race and ethnicity in this question makes it unclear for Iranians whether to write in 'Iranian' under the race category choice of 'Some other race' or to choose to mark 'White' instead" (Fata & Rafii, 2003, p. 5). Moniqua herself spoke of this dilemma.

> I get so confused! I don't know if I should fill out "Asian" or "Other." So I just check off "Asian" or "Other." I don't know what Pacific Islander is! . . . I don't know if I'm that or not. But then I don't know if I should check that or "Other," so sometimes I check that and sometimes I check "Other." I just don't know anymore.

In contrast, Kaliya, one of Moniqua's close friends and the only African American member of the Girls Literacy Discussion Group, in her search for a sense of racial identity, had the support of not only Black parents and siblings but also a large Black extended family and a mostly Black church community. While her interaction with Black peers at school was still limited (African Americans were 5.3% of the student population at Lincoln Middle School), Kaliya had access to Black websites, books, movies, and television shows. Moniqua had few or none of these textual supports in her life.

Aligning herself with her "Hispanic" friends seemed to be a logical choice for Moniqua. She could pass as Hispanic and could find a home with students who "are Hispanic or look Hispanic." Like other women of color, she found a way to navigate the system. Patricia Hill Collins (2009) quoted an elderly Black female domestic worker: "We have always been the best actors in the world. . . . I think that we are much more clever than they are because we know how to play the game. We've always had to live two lives—one for them and one for ourselves" (p. 105). It could be seen as a sign of Moniqua's resiliency that she found a way to assimilate into a culture where she was a small minority. However, this assimilation could also be seen as self-deflating rather than empowering. Unfortunately, there were not spaces in school for Moniqua to examine her choice of racial identification with a critical eye.

Performing a Middle-Class Identity

Erika was a new student at Lincoln Middle School. The second time I met her, she was wearing colored contact lenses whose bright blue contrasted with her brown skin and dark hair. What stood out even more were black letters typed across one of the lenses: TEST.

"I like your contact lenses," I told her.

She smiled a broad, warm smile and said, "Thanks."

"Where did you get them?" I asked.

"At the mall. My mom took me," she told me, without skipping a beat.

That word *TEST* stared out at me and I couldn't keep from asking, "Erika, can you see with that word across your eyeball?"

"If I close one eye I can," she answered, swinging her long hair behind her as she returned to class.

I later learned that Erika's mother did not buy her the contact lenses as she had said. The language arts teacher, Ms. Carpenter, told me later that day that another student had brought several samples of the contact lenses to class and had passed them around to the other students. Ms. Carpenter, fearing students would get eye infections from sharing the contact lenses, made all the students remove the sample lenses. The experience was a foreshadowing of my work with Erika: I learned that watching for the "performance" was just as significant as listening to her words.

Erika had come to Lincoln Middle School from another public middle school across town, placing her in a school environment much different from the one she had left. Her previous school was a high-poverty school with a free lunch rate of 75%, whereas Lincoln Middle School had only

35%. Lincoln Middle School was also much "Whiter" than her previous school, in which, out of its enrollment of nearly 600 students, 91% were students of color: 60% Hispanic, 30% Native American, and 1% African American. In contrast, Lincoln Middle School had over 800 students of whom 54% were White, 34% Hispanic, 6% Native American, 5% Black, and 2% Asian American. Her previous school was in neighborhood that bordered rural areas; the school itself was bordered by an empty lot, failing businesses, small homes, and an open field. On the other hand, Lincoln Middle School had an urban feel to it, being surrounded by busy avenues on two sides.

While Erika had changed schools, she had not changed homes. She still lived in a rural section of town, surrounded by extended family who were, in her words, "Hispanic Catholic" and who had lived in the area for generations. Erika and her brother were brought to school by their grandmother on her way into the city, where she worked cleaning an office building. Erika spent the 40-minute ride curling her hair and applying her makeup. She and her brother arrived at school an hour and a half before the school day officially began.

Over the course of the study, I observed how Erika sometimes, as in the example above, performed a middle-class identity to fit in with her peers. This performance entailed observing the other girls and learning the discourse around her, carefully selecting what to say or not to say, and consciously or unconsciously making immediate and intimate choices about self-presentation. While a young teenager like Erika has very little control over her home environment, which neighborhood she lives in, what type of house, and other economic factors that affect her life circumstances, she does have some control over how she presents those facts to her peers and teachers. She can control what she says and what she omits. These choices represent the performance.

Using performance theory (Butler, 1999), we can understand that class is not only a material location but also a performance and is performative. The material conditions of our lives, such as what economic resources we have access to, are clearly significant in shaping our sense of self. However, we take our material conditions and from their multilayered complexities construct both our inner and outer identities, which are then, usually unconsciously, crafted into a performance. Social class is performative in the sense that there are certain behaviors that, when enacted, can indicate inclusion in or exclusion from a class-based social group. For example, "class-specific styles of speech, such as the use of standard or nonstandard grammar, accents, mannerisms and dress (all of which are racially/ethnically and regionally specific) are learned sets of expressive cultural practices that express class membership" (Bettie,

2003, p. 51). Therefore, the subject can construct her own performance and align herself with one group or another. However, since we are "always performing our cultural identity, the performance is the self" (p. 52). On the other hand, all performances and productions of identity are located within a context of history and culture and broader institutions that assign meanings to race, class, and gender. The following is another example of one of Erika's class performances.

On a spring day, I gave the girls large pieces of white paper and colored markers. The activity was to draw their space at home, whether it was a room or a room they shared; if they lived in more than one home (which a couple of them did), it could be in whichever house they chose. Excited to be drawing, the girls began talking immediately, calling out the colors they needed. "I need purple!" "I need just the black and the white." Erika, as usual, observed before she began, which did not surprise me. Twice when I observed her in class she was copying another student's work. Ms. Carpenter confirmed that she, too, often observed Erika working "off of" the student next to her.

Like the other girls, Erika picked out different-colored markers and began drawing her room: a bed, a closet, a dresser, a window. During this process, the girls were looking at one anothers' pictures and adding more to their own as they heard one another talking. "This is my bed; it's a white comforter." "This is my bed; it's a canopy bed." "That's my VCR and my PS2." "You have a PS2?!" "Yeah, PlayStation." "I have a PS2, too."

The next time I looked at Erika's picture, she had added a TV and a radio. She had also added to her drawing posters of pop stars and pictures of her friends. While other girls had been talking about their pictures, Erika was silent. I asked her about the posters, and she answered in one-word answers.

"OK, I'm totally clueless. Is Ja Rule another band?" I asked.
"Yeah," she replied.
"Who's Nelly, another musician?"
"Yeah."
Kaliya jumped in. "Oh, I have Nelly on my wall too!"
Erika smiled.
"Where do you get the posters?" I asked Erika. But Kaliya, who was submerged in the world of teen hip-hop music, answered for her: "You can get them from the magazines or from the stores."
I tried again. "From the stores? Like which stores?"
Kaliya interjected, "You can get them from . . ."
But Erika finished it off: "Walmart. Kmart."

I asked her about the TV, because by now I had noticed that every
single girl had drawn a TV in her room, some with DVD players.
Erika said that she had a TV with cable in her room. Later I
asked her: "Does your mom have a TV, too, or do you have the
TV?"

She replied, "I have the TV."

One piece of her drawing that later stood out to me was the window. Not
everyone included windows and doors in their drawings. Erika did not
include the door but put in a window, large and centered, bigger than the
bed. The window was drawn as a square divided into four panes with
drooping curtains on each side. (See Figure 3.1.)

Previously, Erika had talked about her bedroom window. In an earlier individual interview, she had spoken about the trailer she lived in
with her mother and younger brother. In talking about her home, Erika
explained that they might move—in her words, "hopefully." She wanted
to move because the trailer, which they had lived in for 4 years, "brings
back so much memories" and because "my window is broken, the outside, because people throw rocks and then I go over there and kicked
their butt. So my window is broken, but we fixed it. Half, not all."

However, the window in Erika's drawing was not broken but had a
perfect square frame with matching curtains. The window in her drawing, in its completeness and perfection down to the details of curtains
pulled to the side, stands as a metaphor for a performance of assimilation. In this group, there was a middle-class norm that pervaded the
group. Even I, as the researcher with my own middle-class background

Figure 3.1. Drawing of Erika's Window

and my own unexamined biases, reinforced this norm by asking the girls to draw their space, thereby assuming that all the girls had a space of their own in the place where they lived. Erika, from a working-poor family living in a trailer in one of the poorer and more rural sections of town, performed a narrative to fit into the constructed group norm.

Erika's drawing reminds me of *The House on Mango Street* (Cisneros, 1989), which Erika listed as one of her favorite books (it was an assigned text she read in a small group in language arts class). A coming-of-age story of a young working-class Chicana girl, the book captures a working-class family longing for upward mobility, for middle-class comforts, for a dream house without a broken window or a door that jams.

> They always told us that one day we would move into a house, a real house that would be ours forever and we wouldn't have to move each year. And our house would have running water and pipes that worked. And inside it would have real stairs, not hallway stairs but stairs inside like the houses on TV. And we'd have a basement and at least three washrooms so when we took a bath we wouldn't have to tell everybody. Our house would be white with trees around it, a great big yard and grass growing without a fence. This was the house Papa talked about when he held a lottery ticket and this was the house Mama dreamed up in the stories she told us before we went to bed. (Cisneros, 1989, p. 4)

I believe that Erika enjoyed this text because it was one of the few times in the language arts classroom that she could see part of her own reality, longings, and experiences reflected back to her from a page in a book. In an interview about her writing, Cisneros said that her intent in writing *The House on Mango Street* was "to write stories that don't get told—my mother's stories, my students' stories, the stories of women in the neighborhood, the stories of all those people who don't have the ability to document their lives" (Satz, 1997, p. 1). Erika's story is one of those stories, the stories that do not come to voice on the page within a mainstream setting. Her story is one that slips between the cracks, lives and breathes beneath the surface, and is invisible in the formal school setting.

A Queer, White, Geek Identity Performance

As a queer student, Tetra, who identified herself as butch and a lesbian, was an outlier at Lincoln Middle School. Heavy-set with dark hair, pale skin, and black-rimmed glasses, Tetra knew that she looked different from most of the other girls in her 8th-grade classes. In a group writing exercise, Tetra wrote, "If you saw me on the outside you'd think. . . . I'm an outcast or maybe a druggie with straight Fs. That's what one of my friends thought when you only see the outside." As a lesbian, Tetra had faced harassment from her middle school peers. "When I came out, last year, in 7th grade," she explained, "all these people started flipping out and saying, 'Stay away from her. She's the gay one! You'll catch it!'"

Tetra situated herself in the Girls Literacy Discussion Group as the "oddball," different from the other girls. I noticed Tetra's separation from the other girls right away. From the first group meeting, Tetra was set apart. When we entered our meeting space, an empty science lab, the girls all sat in a row except for Tetra, who sat one row ahead of everyone else, one row closer to me. When I gave my opening presentation about how we're all different and how we're going to come together as one group, at the word *different* Erika pointed at Tetra behind her back and made a face to the girl sitting next to her. Tetra didn't seem to notice. For example, in one writing exercise, Tetra filled in the blank: "I am . . ." with "Tetra Perry. I am a musician, a teen, an artist, a thinker, and most likely an oddball." At another point, she said, "Forever and forever I'll still be a weird little oddball person. . . . I don't think *oddball* is a bad term. I don't think *freak* is either. It's just another word to describe me."

In addition to her queer identity, Tetra also identified as a "geek," "a band geek," and "preppy." For Tetra, this aspect of her identity included participating in band, excelling at computers, and generally doing well in school. Her identification with the "geek" identity was also an oppositional identity formation. This identification as "different" is not uncommon in nerd youth culture. Mary Bucholtz (1999), in her study of nerd girls, noted that "nerds in U.S. high schools are not socially isolated misfits but competent members of a distinctive and oppositionally defined community of practice" (p. 211). Likewise, Tetra was not socially isolated; she was surrounded by her "geek" friends who positioned themselves in opposition to the popular students.

Literacy is one arena where geeks, or nerds, typically assert their opposition (Eglash, 2002), as was the case with Tetra. In the history of the nerd identity, a nerd was typically a White male who showed intense interest in and often mastery of science and math. More recently, nerd identity has developed an association with what Eglash (2002) called a "techno-cultural identity" which includes a significant technological expertise (p. 60). This interest in computers, science, and science fiction texts is posited in opposition to an interest in beauty, social conformity, and physical agility. Furthermore, the nerd, like the "preppy," has an interest in doing well in school and with school-based texts.

Tetra embraced this "geek" identity, which situated her in opposition to the other girls in the group, and used her literacies as a way to express her opposition. While the other girls liked teen magazines, Tetra hated them. While the other girls liked pop music, she liked classical. While the other girls used the Internet to send e-mail or look up their horoscopes or their favorite musicians, she used the Internet to read fan fiction. While the other girls read real-life drama, she read *Harry Potter* and *The Hobbit*. While the other girls chatted with one another, she focused on finishing her homework.

Many of the literacy preferences of nerds, including Tetra, focus on performing an intellectual and technological superiority or mastery. "Many positive identity practices in which nerds engage contribute to the display of intelligence. The community value placed on intelligence is reflected in non-linguistic identity practices oriented to the world of school, books and knowledge" (Bucholtz, 1999, p. 214). For example, Tetra was the only student in the Girls Literacy Discussion Group to talk in a group discussion about going into honors classes in high school. She identified her social group as "good students" who "like school," and she said that standardized tests are "important" and low grades make her "really, really sad."

By emphasizing intellect rather than femininity, nerd identity, for a tomboy like Tetra, also provided a relief from heteronormative femininity. Bucholtz (1999) found in her study that "for girls, nerd identity offers an alternative to the pressures of hegemonic femininity—an ideological construct that is at best incompatible with and at worst, hostile to female intellectual ability" (p. 213). Nerd identity gave Tetra a way to resist femininity and heteronormative social expectations. For example, in one of the group discussions, the girls were talking about teen magazines and whether they allowed the advertising in them to influence their fashion decisions. Tetra was quiet for a while and then started playing with her glasses, the black-rimmed glasses that are often depicted in the stereotypical nerd image. In the middle of the girls' heated discussion about whether they were more likely to wear something that a friend recommended or that they saw in a magazine, Tetra piped in, "Can anyone pop a lens back into eyeglasses?" Tetra interrupted a conversation that centered on hegemonic femininity with a concrete image of nerd identity—the glasses. However, her resistance was barely noted. The other girls responded by ignoring her and continuing with their conversation.

Interestingly enough, although Tetra, who was White, framed herself as the most advanced in terms of technological skills and ability, Kaliya, who was African American, was, in fact, much more sophisticated in terms of digital literacy. For example, Tetra said, "I love the computer. I get on every single day, and on Sundays I spend the entire day on the computer." Kaliya, on the other hand, never mentioned any interest in computers or technology, but on the day I took the group to the computer lab, I saw that Kaliya was clearly the most comfortable and adept with technological literacies of all the girls. She quickly checked her e-mail, scanned photos to send to her cousin, listened to music on the Internet on her headphones, and downloaded images of her favorite musicians—all at the same time and within minutes. O'Brian (2006) calls this literacy practice multimediating, explaining that "multimediators move seamlessly in and out of the real and virtual worlds, rapidly and automatically using various technologies that they embrace as extensions of themselves" (p. 36). When I asked Kaliya about her computer literacy skills, she explained, "[My mom's] really into computers. She works at [a science center]. She's a computer person. She builds computers." As much as Kaliya and her family demonstrated technological mastery, Kaliya never mentioned it as part of her self-identity.

This irony points to the fact that nerd identity performance is not only "counter-hegemonic" but also steeped in Whiteness (Bucholtz, 1999, p. 214). Eglash (2002) links nerd identity to race and posits that it is associated exclusively with White culture or "acting White." The history of nerd or geek identity has been one that is both gendered and racialized as White and male. These stereotypes are located within a broader racialized context where, on the one hand, Blacks are stereotyped as the "anti-nerds" and, on the other hand, Asian Americans are steeped in "compulsory nerdiness" (Eglash, 2002, p. 58). Perhaps Kaliya rarely mentioned her use of technology because, as an African American girl, she saw a technological identity as not only "uncool" but also as White and male.

Therefore, by identifying with nerd or geek identity, Tetra was aligning herself not only with a counter-hegemonic culture that resists normative femininity and social conformity but also with a culture that embraces its White privilege. Tetra was the only White girl in the Girls Literacy Discussion Group. While many White students her age might be oblivious to their racial and ethnic group membership (Tatum, 2003), Tetra had some awareness of her Whiteness. In one of the first group meetings, Tetra identified herself as both "White" and "Greco-Roman." When discussing race, she revealed that most of her friends were White. She explained about the "band geeks," her self-identified social group: "We're more of a very White group. There's Ishmael. Ishmael hangs out with us all of the time but he's like one of the very few people that's not White." Later she added:

I realize one of the reasons that we [my friends and I] are mainly White people is that it might be because the people in the group are extremely preppy. We're like the preppy White kids. I don't really see so many preppy Black people or preppy Hispanics or Asian people. I don't see that. Except for Ishmael; he's very preppy. He is! If he gets a really high A, like a 99.9%, in the class, he starts crying because he thinks he has a bad grade.

Tetra equated the term *preppy* with trying to do well in school, which, in turn, she equated with Whiteness. She had internalized the message that White students do better in school than students of color. Although her teachers worked hard to dispel racial stereotypes and promote racial equality, Tetra was educated within a broader educational system that still, on some level, promotes and models such inequalities. For example, at Lincoln Middle School, of approximately 50 regular education teachers, only three were people of color. Both administrators were White, blonde women. In contrast, nearly all of the support staff (janitorial, cafeteria, educational assistants, and secretaries) were people of color. Such modeling is not lost on students.

Studies of urban public schools have documented the racial and economic tracking that is reproduced in schools with diverse populations (Brantlinger, 2003; Kelly, 2008; Lopez, 2003; Oakes, 2005, 2008). Other studies have indicated that in diverse public schools like Lincoln Middle School, parents of White middle-class students try to help their children maintain a competitive academic advantage by pushing for their involvement in activities such as band or orchestra, tracking them into honors or gifted classrooms, or making sure they are placed with the "right" teachers (Lareau, 2008; Maier, Ford, & Schneider, 2008; Oakes, 2008). "White and/or wealthy, well-educated, and politically powerful parents" demand differentiation for their children and are "subtle and savvy in their resistance to detracking efforts that lead to desegregation within schools" (Wells & Oakes, 1996, p. 138). The result is that these activities and programs are White spaces within an otherwise racially diverse public school setting. For example, the school data listed the "Hispanic" population at Lincoln Middle School as 34% and the "Anglo" population as 54%, but the teacher of the gifted program said that there were only 2 "Hispanic" students (15%) and 26 "Anglo" students (86%) in that program. Such inequality demonstrates racial tracking in a diverse public school.

For Tetra, attending a public school where close to half her class were students of color and many of those were the most popular students, her nerd identity helped her maintain, perhaps unconsciously, a superior position steeped in Whiteness and class privilege. Just as the label "gifted" allows a student to separate him- or herself from the masses, by being a "nerd," Tetra also separated herself from the rest of the students. By embracing this geek or nerd identity, supported by her literacy performances, Tetra could maintain White privilege in a racially diverse environment.

As a tomboy, a fat girl, and a lesbian, Tetra held very little social capital in the larger student world of Lincoln Middle School outside of her
clique of "geeks." But social capital in the larger hegemonic society is different from that in the student world at Lincoln Middle School. Tetra, by
identifying and performing an identity as a "band geek," could, perhaps
unconsciously, maintain a position that was both racially and economically privileged by society at large. On some level, Tetra knew that being a
lesbian cost her social capital, but being White and middle class gave her
some privilege in the larger hegemonic society.

IMPLICATIONS AND RECOMMENDATIONS

Students come to school to learn and, in a sense, to change. "Schools exist to change young people. The young people should be different—better—for their experience there" (Sizer & Sizer, 1999, p. 103). The formal
lessons teachers teach are only a fraction of what students learn in school.
The hidden curriculum, including lessons about race, class, gender, and
sexuality, is a dominant part of what middle school girls learn in school
each day. These race and class performances are part of the unexamined
hidden curriculum at Lincoln Middle School.

As teachers, we must address the issues taught by the hidden curriculum or the youth culture of the school will do it for us. Coupled with
the unexamined issues we as teachers pass on unconsciously through
our words, deeds, and attitudes, the youth culture may reinforce or in-
troduce lessons that are filled with misinformation, misjudgment, bias,
or discrimination.

Tetra, Erika, and Moniqua, like other middle school students, are
grappling with issues of race, class, gender, and sexuality and how these
identities play out in their lives. The classroom should be a setting where
students can examine issues of power and performance, question social
norms, and visualize positive changes in their representations of self. After all, "thinking hard—grappling—in an informed and careful way is the
most likely route to a principled and constructive life" (Sizer & Sizer, 1999,
p. 38). Schools can be a space to provide structures for this informed and
careful grappling.

However, teachers are often afraid to create spaces for such conversations about difficult and potentially controversial topics. "Few schools
place a high value on questioning, even though it is the habit which is
most likely to lead to consequential scholarship and responsible adulthood" (Sizer & Sizer, 1999, p. 37). Teachers are afraid of conversations
getting out of hand, of feeling uncomfortable, and of managing opposing

opinions about sensitive issues. Many teachers "fear losing control in a classroom where there is no one way to approach a subject—only multiple ways and multiple references" (hooks, 1994, p. 36). Topics like race and class performances have no right or wrong answers—the significance lies in allowing students to probe how they are performing race, class, and gender and why. These conversations are much more ambiguous and potentially controversial than a banking approach to education.

Teachers are also afraid that if they open up the classroom to examine students' lives, then they won't cover the course material they are obligated to teach. As one teacher said, "What do you mean build relationships? My job is to teach history" (quoted in Easton, 2008, p. 19). Teachers need to learn how to facilitate conversations that can provoke examination and reflection while maintaining a respectful classroom environment. Teachers can learn how to cover content as well as the significant questions in students' lives.

Students also need to learn how to participate in such conversations and dialogues. Like the need for critical media literacy skills, students need to learn the skills of critical literacy, or looking at the world from a critical and transformative perspective. In general, such discourses usually take place at the university level—in sociology, anthropology, American studies, gender studies, women's studies, and education departments—but do not trickle down to the middle school level.

What would it be like to sit with Tetra and prod her to examine why almost all of her friends are White? Or for Moniqua and Erika to discuss why all of their friends are other students of color? There is the opportunity for a truly transformative experience if students were to sit together and examine how issues like race and class play a role in their everyday social world. In those conversations, and only in those conversations, are the seeds of real change.

CHAPTER 4

Critical Media Literacy for a Text-Saturated World

Researchers have referred to this era as the age of media saturation, media bombardment, information flood, and data smog (De Abreu, 2007; Gill 2007; Potter, 2004; Shenk, 1997). For all of the girls in the Girls Literacy Discussion Group, movies and television were ever-present background influences in their worlds. Every single participant said that she had a television in her bedroom, and most of them had DVD players as well.

Given the enormous role of mass media in the lives of adolescents, examination of these texts is now central to any understanding of adolescent literacy. The current literature on adolescent literacy focuses on the significance of multiple forms of texts, including popular culture, in the lives of adolescents (Alvermann et al., 2006; Christenbury, Bomer, & Smagorinsky, 2009; Hagood, 2009; Mahiri, 2004). Current research calls for breaking down the walls between in-school and out-of-school texts, including media and digital texts, as these distinctions are no longer salient. "In recognizing the vast presence of media in adolescents' lives, there needs to be an acceptance of media texts as having legitimacy in academic curricula" (Bruce, 2009, p. 300). The girls' experiences at Lincoln Middle School echo these findings.

In my research, the girls demonstrated multiple approaches to media texts. At times, they were consumers of media text, values, and cultural stories without critical analysis. On other occasions they sharply examined texts with a critical eye, demonstrating significant critical literacy skills. Sometimes they used media texts to support their identities. Sometimes they actively resisted the messages embedded in the texts. There were instances when they investigated multiple layers of meaning found in the text and other times when they absorbed media messages without questioning their perspectives, the creators' motives, or the implications. There was an ongoing interactive process between media text and reader that shifted with context, content, and timing, influencing the girls' ability to be active agents in their own process of meaning-making.

TEEN MAGAZINES AND GENDER EXPRESSION

One of the main texts that the girls liked to read was teen magazines. One day I brought a stack of teen magazines to the Girls Literacy Discussion Group. There was a mad dash as they grabbed a magazine of their choice off the table. Hurt feelings ensued when the faster girls got the more desirable magazines.

Research has indicated that teen magazines play a role in the social construction of femininity, concepts of beauty, and body image (Driver, 2007; Duke & Kreshel, 1998; Hall, 2011; Kaplan & Cole, 2000; McRobbie, 2000). Driver (2007) refers to teen magazines as "distinct girl genres that work to prescribe beauty and romantic idealizations" (p. 129). As a text, teen magazines send a message of what it means to be a teen girl in our society. As a girl constructs a sense of self, these textual messages play a role in her meaning-making of self.

When asked why they liked reading teen magazines, the girls mentioned that the magazines covered topics of interest to them in a format that was easy to read or flip through. "When you read the articles that are in there, they're kind of fun," explained Erika. "They have a lot of people with experience in there, like, stories and stuff and you can learn from that," added Angela.

Overall, the common appeal of the magazines was their assumed connection to the real-life experiences of the girls. The girls stated that they liked the teen magazines because they covered topics that they cared about, including personal stories of struggles with family, friends, and boyfriends; fashion ideas; dating tips; and information on bodies and sexuality. "It's like a teenage book," Kaliya described.

Tetra was the only girl in the group who said that she was not interested in reading teen magazines. Tetra explained that she didn't like teen magazines because they were too focused on beauty and fashion. Given the amount of material in teen magazines devoted to either femininity or heteronormativity, her response was not surprising (Driver, 2007; Duke & Kreshel, 1998; Hall, 2011; Mazzarella & Pecora, 1999). "Magazines work as an intense site for shaping normative investments in heterosexual femininity" (Driver, 2007, p. 129). As a lesbian/bisexual and a tomboy, Tetra rejected conventional forms of femininity and heteronormativity. Tetra explained, "I don't care about my hair. I don't care about makeup. If I find it and it smells clean and it looks clean, I'm going to wear it. I don't care. Almost everyone I know really well is like that, too." In keeping with her sense of self, Tetra rejected the teen magazines and the images of womanhood they presented, indicating a use of her critical literacies and a resistance to these "oppressive cultural stories" (Oliver, 1999, p. 221).

In contrast, the other girls reflected a spectrum of relationships to both normative femininity and teen magazines. For example, Kaliya liked getting fashion ideas from the magazines. Based on both appearance and words, Kaliya and Moniqua seemed to be the girls most interested in mainstream fashion. Kaliya switched her hairstyle several times throughout the semester from braids to straightened hair to a styled cut. Her clothes always looked carefully selected and matched, and I never saw her wearing just jeans and a sweatshirt like some of the other girls. Kaliya said that she used the magazines to get ideas for new styles that would make her stand out among the other girls. She saw the magazines as a tool that would give her a fashion advantage. She explained:

> I try to do my own style, but it doesn't always work. Like I got this really cute pink skirt the other day, and I thought I was the only person who had it. Then I went to the Sand Dune [an underage dance club] and I saw two other girls with the same skirt but in different colors. So I have to go take it back . . . and I was going to wear it that night! I would have looked stupid!

On several occasions Kaliya also linked both fashion choices and magazine choices to her favorite musicians. She explained:

> If I see B2K on it, I'll grab it right away. Or if I see Chingy on it, I'll buy it right away. Yesterday I went to Music World to go get movies and right away I see B2K, right? So I picked up the magazine and I started reading it and my dad bought it for me. Like every time I see B2K on a magazine, I always get it. I love B2K. When I see magazines with singers on it, I'll get it.

Both Kaliya and Moniqua noted that they might find an outfit that they liked in a magazine but that their choices were limited to what they could find in the local mall. "The things you see on TV [or in a magazine] are clothes they don't really sell in stores," lamented Moniqua.

"In this town," finished Kaliya.

On the other hand, Angela and Chris, like Tetra, claimed that they did not read magazines for fashion ideas. "The way I dress, I think, it doesn't depend on what I see in a magazine or what other people wear. I think it's what I'm comfortable with. It's what I like," explained Angela. Angela and Chris both stated that they did read teen magazines but that they read them for the stories. Angela shared with the group an article she had read in one of the teen magazines about a girl helping a suicidal friend as an example of the kind of stories she liked to read in teen magazines. "I thought it was really touching. It touched me," Angela told the group.

Likewise, Chris asserted that "[teen magazines] are not just about beauty and all that stuff, but they have lots of tips on everything, and some magazines like that one have real-life stories. Sometimes you can learn from other people's experiences, like how they really do connect, how they are like us and not like us."

Tetra, Chris, and Angela all stated that they did not use the magazines for fashion ideas. These three girls were all also the members of social groups that were the least invested in maintaining a highly feminized appearance. Compared to the other three girls, Tetra, Chris, and Angela chose gender expressions that were more androgynous than feminine. Chris, who played on the school basketball team, often wore sports clothes. Tetra and Angela both usually wore gender-neutral clothes like sweatshirts and loose jeans. All three girls had simple hairstyles and wore little or no makeup. On the other hand, Kaliya, Moniqua, and Erika wore their hair in highly stylized fashions, always wore makeup, and often wore jewelry and feminized fashion choices such as mini-skirts, midriff shirts, and tight pants, much like those in the teen magazines.

An examination of sociocultural background and experience can help contextualize the various girls' responses to both the magazines and femininity. As mentioned earlier, girls create their expressions of gender and femininity based not only on written or visual texts such as magazines or television but also on their "linguistic-experiential reservoir," or life experiences (Rosenblatt, 1994). Girls perform "different versions of femininity that are integrally linked to and inseparable from their class and racial/ ethnic performances" (Bettie, 2003, p. 5). Therefore, it is probably not a coincidence that Moniqua, Kaliya, and Erika, all girls of color, had a different perspective on fashion and femininity than Angela, Chris, and Tetra, who were of different races but all performed middle-class identities.

Likewise, Tetra made it clear that her approach to fashion was aligned with that of her social group, a nearly exclusively White group of students who played in the band. She said:

> Most of the girls I hang out with and women I hang out with, even my mom, don't care about their hair. If they wake up and their hair is sticking straight up, they're going to try and control it, but if it takes longer than 2 minutes, then too bad, it's just going to be that way and if anyone else is annoyed, that's their problem. . . . We don't care about hair or makeup.

Interestingly, Moniqua, Erika, and Kaliya's group was differentiated from other peer groups not only by style but also by specific consumer products, such as brand names or particular stores. For example, I asked the girls, "If someone came from outer space or another country, what would they have to do or look like to fit into your group of friends at Lincoln Middle School?"

Kaliya was the first to answer, "They have to shop at mostly stores . . ."

"At the mall," interrupted Moniqua.

"Like Rave and 5-7-9, and they have to wear makeup and probably color their hair," finished Kaliya.

The brand names and names of particular stores and styles are texts that adolescents read and must make meaning of each day. The naming of certain "popular" stores linked consumer culture to their youth culture. It also linked hegemonic fashion displays of femininity to youth culture at Lincoln Middle School. In order to fit into that particular social group, girls needed to perform a normative femininity that included wearing makeup, wearing certain clothes, and doing one's hair in a certain current fashion. When I asked Moniqua if you could get kicked out of her group if you wore totally outrageous clothes, she answered, "You wouldn't be in the group."

In these cases, the girls did not indicate any resistance to the lure of the corporate fashion industry, nor did they indicate any recognition or awareness that they were part of a larger capitalist design aimed at feeding corporate interests. Youth culture and consumer fashion were implicitly linked without questioning. The connections between youth culture and consumer fashion and the infiltration of the corporate world into adolescent peer groups have been noted as problematic by educators and media studies scholars. Mahiri (2004) reports on how the corporate world "commodifies messages and images from youth culture for global consumption while educators often disdain the use of popular cultural materials in schools" (p. 3). Youth culture in many ways has become so indistinguishable from consumer culture that without sophisticated media literacy skills, young people are not going to be able to analyze or begin to counteract these corporate messages.

The texts of the corporate consumer market not only played a role in differentiating social groups, it also played a role in the girls' of sense of self. For example, in an activity in the beginning of the Girls Literacy Discussion Group, the girls met in pairs and introduced themselves to each other. Then they reported back to the group what they had learned about their partners. I had listed on the board some sample questions for the girls to ask each other, such as: How old are you? What do you like to do for fun? What religion are you? All of the girls, on their own, added some aspect of mass media, and some of them included consumer culture in their responses. For example, here is what Chris said she had learned about Angela:

That's Angela, and her favorite movie is *Finding Nemo*. Her hobby is playing on the computer and hanging out with her friends. Her favorite food is spaghetti. She was born on May 18th, which is the date after mine. She was born in this state, and her favorite sport is basketball, and she shops at American Eagle, Packsack, Industrial, and Zumi.

Angela's identification with the stores where she buys her clothes not only links her to a particular social group; it also indicates a sense of herself within the school youth culture. For Angela, her sense of self was affiliated with the stores she patronizes. Likewise, when Moniqua and Erika described each other, they listed whether they preferred Coke or Pepsi in their self-descriptions. These examples indicate how branding interacts with adolescent identities. "In contemporary culture, brands are embedded within social relations . . . brand equity is crafted through building brand identities and personalities that come alive within the social space and the imagination of consumers" (Carah, 2010, p. 4). Through this branding process, corporations infiltrate youth cultures and identities, ultimately influencing girls' senses of self.

MASS MEDIA AND CRITICAL LITERACY

At times, the girls accepted media messages without question; at other times they demonstrated sophisticated critical media literacy skills. Here's an example of the latter. This is an excerpt of their discussion from a day when the group was watching a clip from a music video:

"If you really want to sell something and you really want to make it popular, you either have to have a lot of violence in it or—" began Tetra.
"A lot of naked people," interrupted Moniqua.
"Or you have to have a lot of references to sex," continued Tetra.
"And drugs," interjected Moniqua.
"Because sex sells," explained Tetra. "Most of the time they're not going to have guys doing that. If someone had a guy doing anything close to what they have girls do in these videos, they'd probably get sued and all these people would write them hate letters, but with the girls, you know, it's OK. They're just women."

In this example, they are demonstrating critical literacy. "Critical literacy refers to an awareness that the language of texts and the reader's responses to it are not neutral but are shaped by social contexts and our experiences as people of particular races, ethnicities, genders, and social classes" (Young, 2001, p. 5). Furthermore, critical literacy includes examinations of how texts can either reinforce hegemonic ideas of power and privilege or work to create transformation in the world or both. While past research paints a picture of adolescent girls as just "vulnerable targets of detrimental media images of femininity" (Durham, 1999, p. 193), I found that the girls were, at least sometimes, agents of meaning-making, often with a sophisticated critical eye.

Tetra, in particular, voiced strong opinions about media texts:

> I think that most models they put in the magazines try to make other women and girls and everyone want to wear that makeup and those clothes. They're just grouping everyone into a certain group, and I know that. My mom gets this fashion magazine, and I can't look through it because every time I do, there are people in there assuming that I wear makeup. They assume that I wear suits and dresses. They assume that because this person looks this way, I'm going to want to look that way. They try too hard. They don't look like real people because they're just too thin. They're too thin, they're too beautiful, they're too whatever; they don't look like real people. They're like dolls, mannequins.

As an adolescent tomboy, Tetra has probably done more thinking about normative femininity and how it is reproduced than the other girls. Judith Halberstam (1998) wrote about the experiences of adolescent girls who resist compulsory femininity, or tomboys, which she defines as "an extended period of female masculinity" (p. 5). According to Halberstam, adolescence, for girls, is a time of extreme pressure toward gender conformity, and "it is in the context of female adolescence that the tomboy instincts of millions of girls are remodeled into compliant forms of femininity. That any girls do emerge at the end of adolescence as masculine women is quite amazing" (p. 6). It seems to me that Tetra, a young woman who self-identified as a tomboy, was turning away from teen magazines in an attempt of resistance to compulsory femininity. Her words and actions indicated a use of her critical literacies to embody a critical analysis.

Interestingly enough, the other strongest critic in the group of how normative femininity is represented in the media was Moniqua, who was on the opposite extreme of gender expression from Tetra. While Tetra was a tomboy who never wore makeup or jewelry, only wore pants and shirts, and could pass as a young man, Moniqua said that she did not feel comfortable even inside her own house if she was not wearing makeup and that she spent many hours looking in the mirror, focusing on her feminized appearance. But Tetra and Moniqua were similar in their outspoken critiques of how girls and women are represented in the media, including magazines. Moniqua brought a race consciousness to the analysis as well.

"In movies, like drama movies, how come minority people are always the ones dropping out and getting pregnant?! Why? Stupid! Haven't you noticed?" Moniqua pointed out. Here Moniqua indicated her awareness of how race and gender are coupled together in the mass media to create stereotypes that scapegoat women of color. Girls of color are stereotyped as "hypersexual, bad, and poor," while White girls are stereotyped as "middle class, asexual, and good" (Tolman, 2005, p. 171). These stereotypes, based on race, class, and gender, underlie media images of female sexuality. Moniqua drew attention to these stereotypes in her critiques of media images.

Likewise, Kaliya raised the issue of how African Americans are portrayed in the media. "We'll be watching a movie, like say it's a scary movie and my brother, he'll be like, 'Dude! The Black person gets killed! How come the Black person has to die first?! See, look, he's White! He's going toward the action!'" As girls of color, Moniqua and Kaliya voiced awareness of how these stereotypes are reproduced in the media and, in doing so, were resisting these oppressive cultural narratives. This is part of developing literacy. After all, "to be literate is not to be free, it is to be present and active in the struggle for reclaiming one's voice, history and present" (Freire & Macedo, 1987, p. 11). Students of color need more spaces where they can develop such critical literacies.

The girls not only critiqued the media but also noticed some of the connections between mass media culture and local youth culture. "Some girls dress like that at the Sand Dune" noted Kaliya, referring to the women in the video and a local under-21 dance club.

"Yeah," agreed Erika. "And the guys are all over them!"

Moniqua made the connection between the media images and the pressure for girls to dress like the images they see in the media. "[Girls] watch those videos and then they'll be like, 'Oh well, for me to get attention, I'm going to have to look like that.'"

The girls also saw that the media puts pressure on boys to conform to a physical standard as well. The girls listed pressure on boys to be "buff," "outdoorsy," "like football," "masculine," and "sexually experienced." Moniqua explained, "I think that they do feel pressure because, oh my God, have you ever heard guys complain about their haircuts! You don't even have hair! What are you talking about?! I think it's interesting how they get haircuts all the time!" She laughed.

However, the girls overwhelmingly believed that the pressure on girls was more intense than the pressure on boys to be masculine. "I think girls feel a lot more pressure than they do because what we worry about, a lot more, having kids, first of all. And then all that stereotypical stuff about being 'hos' and being put in all those videos," explained Moniqua, more somber now.

"I agree with Moniqua," added Tetra. "I think that guys have some pressure to look good but if they don't, they don't have to. . . . With a girl, there's way more pressure to be beautiful and sexual." In this sense, the girls were acutely aware of the gender differences in attitude toward bodies.

The girls also displayed critical analysis when they discussed how girls' bodies are policed by use of the label "ho" to stigmatize girls who defied the group norms regarding sexual behavior, attitude, and dress. For example, Kaliya stated, "You know what I don't get? A girl could go and do something with a boy, like kiss them or go out with them and then go out with another guy and kiss them and go out with another guy and then you're a "ho"! But a guy can go out with her and her and her . . .''

Erika interrupted. "And they go out with like 12 girls and they don't get called a 'ho' or a 'slut.' They just get, 'Oh, well, whatever. Nice pimping dude!'"

Later, the girls named it as they saw it. "See guys are supposed to be more sexually experienced," explained Tetra. "But if the woman is more sexually experienced."

"She's a 'ho'!" interrupted Erika.

"She's a 'ho'! Yeah, exactly!" repeated Moniqua.

The term *ho* is clearly drawn from the larger mass media, as the girls pointed out how the term appears in music videos to label women. Just as the girls criticized the practice of labeling women as "hos" in the media, they criticized the same practice when it was repeated by their peers. Other researchers have noted that historically terms like *ho* or *slut* have been used exclusively for girls as a term "adopted to label and curtail girls' behavior and movement" (Bloustien, 2004, p. 94). The term *ho* was used by the peer culture at Lincoln Middle School to put limits on girls' behavior in a way that is different from what is expected from boys. In their own language, the girls were able to articulate the gender biases underlying these comments.

At one point in our discussions, the girls also demonstrated critical feminist analysis on the issue of girls and body image. "Girls have the pressure of hair, clothes, makeup, and all that stuff and guys mainly worry about their body and being fit. And if they're not fit, it's still OK," explained Tetra.

"People will still like him," added Moniqua. "Fat girls get more crap than fat guys do."

The girls indicated that the dominant school narrative demanded that girls must be thin in order to be accepted in the peer social world. Girls who did not conform to this compulsory thinness were punished in the school youth culture. "People call us pigs and fatties," Tetra reported sadly.

"Nobody really likes fat girls," agreed Moniqua.

"I've never seen a girl go up to a guy and be like, 'You're fat and you need to lose weight!' But I've seen guys do that to girls," Angela explained.

"It always happens to girls," affirmed Moniqua.

"A guy will go up to a girl and say, 'You're fat'?" I asked for clarification.

"You're fat," said Moniqua.

"You're fat," repeated Angela.

"You need to lose weight," added Erika.

"A guy came up to me and said I was obese," shared Tetra. "A guy in this school."

At Lincoln Middle School, the term *fat* was an insult used by both boys and girls exclusively against girls. Girls would use the term against another girl "if they didn't like them." Erika explained, "They'll go up to each other and say: 'You're fat!' 'You need to lose weight!' 'Stupid fat bitch!'"

This phenomenon of policing the size of girls' bodies is an example of how a text message obtained from the media, parents, and other cultural influences is passed down. The students at Lincoln Middle School did not invent such pressure to be thin. Ideal body weight is socially constructed and varies from culture to culture. A particular cultural message is handed to the youth, and the youth toss it back and forth to one another. When it's held, it sinks into the skin and becomes part of one's sense of self without even realizing where it has come from or when it became part of the self.

Despite the fact that they critiqued cultural media messages around body image, it also seemed that they had few tools for resistance. The girls expressed contradictory responses to the pressure to be thin and to conform to a normative definition of beauty. For example, at the time, there was an increase on television of reality shows focusing on plastic surgery as a route to achieve an idealized body, with titles such as *The Swan* and *Extreme Makeover*. The girls discussed these shows and were overwhelmingly opposed to the concept of plastic surgery.

"I think God made you that way, so you should keep your image. I don't think you should change it," explained Kaliya.

Angela agreed with her. "I think that God made you look like you are, like the way that you are, for a reason."

Moniqua had a different perspective. "I don't think that God made you that way. I think that your DNA made you that way." Yet she agreed that plastic surgery was unnecessary. "It's stupid. How happy can they be?" Likewise, Angela, in an individual interview, explained:

All you see on TV now is the little skinny girls. Whenever they see that, they want to be exactly like that so they go and become bulimic or anorexic. They want to go and have plastic body surgery to look exactly like that person. But if here was like somebody real famous who was like an average size, you know, not all skinny and stuff, I'm sure that people would feel so much better about themselves.

Yet the girls also expressed disappointment with their own bodies and the desire to be thinner. For example, in a writing exercise, Tetra wrote: "I have to remind myself to stop calling me fat or stupid." Similarly, Angela wrote: "If I could change one thing about myself or my life I'd . . . want to be skinny because that's the one thing I hate about myself."

IMPLICATIONS AND RECOMMENDATIONS

Media and its centrality in our lives is here to stay, and girls need tools to learn how to better use media as a positive influence in their lives. "For better or for worse, media is a major force in the lives of adolescents. There is no question that it is a curriculum that socializes and works to shape young people's worldview" (Hall, 2011, p. 18). Media is "our children's window and mirror, showing them a world beyond their own backyards and offering them a reflection of the lives they lead" (Cahn, Kalagian, & Lyon, 2011, p. 46). Media, as a text that is central to girls' lives and their meaning-making, needs to be recognized as a major literacy text, one that teachers are obligated to address in the classroom.

While the girls in my study had access to an incredible amount of information and a cacophony of voices and messages about femininity, womanhood, sexuality, and the female body, from sources such as Internet web pages, reality TV, and teen magazines, they lacked spaces to process and explore the meanings of these texts. They also lacked facilitation by teachers to further develop the critical thinking skills related to critical media literacy.

The Girls Literacy Discussion Group, formed as part of my research investigations, was one of the few spaces in school where the girls felt that they could talk about media and its impact on their lives. I was surprised by the extent of critical analysis that they demonstrated. Though many studies present adolescent girls as passive recipients of media messages, I found that these girls exhibited multiple approaches to media texts. While at times they seemed to passively accept media narratives, there were other times when they were critical, rejected and resisted oppressive texts, and embraced texts that fed their subjective constructions of self.

In this way, the Girls Literacy Discussion Group acted as a form of action research—the girls were engaging in a learning process at the same time that the group was functioning as a research site. In the group, they voiced strong emotions regarding media texts. Their intense reactions as well as the way they often pulled group discussions back to topics related to the media are just two indications of the need for more spaces in the school setting to analyze the media texts that surround adolescents. Researchers have proposed that for girls, the need for critical media literacy skills is especially significant. Based on her study of adolescent girls, Oliver (1999) stated that "the oppressive cultural stories and images that girls are confronted with daily require them to have the ability to critically examine these images and stories if they are to become healthy women" (p. 223). These skills are also essential for students of color: "Due to a lack of robust learning opportunities, many youth of color do not develop the critical literacy skills that would enable them to critique their own experiences" (Winn, 2011, p. 110). Schools need to provide these spaces for critical examination.

This research speaks to the need for further development of critical media literacy skills in the middle school classroom. These girls, like all middle school students, were just at the beginning of a period in their cognitive development when they could begin to understand on a deeper level the complicated and complex messages they received from the world around them. They were actively engaging with the texts in a complicated, complex, and sometimes even contradictory process of meaning-making. Media literacy provides students with the opportunities to develop the skills needed to adequately make sense of the flood of texts that pervade their lives.

According to De Abreu (2007), there are five core concepts embedded in media literacy development. They include understanding that all media messages are constructed, media messages use creative language, different people experience the same media differently,and media messages are embedded with values and a point of view and are constructed to gain profit and/or power (pp. 7–10). Media literacy skills require analysis and evaluation, higher-order thinking skills that teachers can help their students develop. Students can be taught specific techniques to critique media texts, such as content analysis, semiotics, and discourse analysis.

Critical media literacy takes the concept of media one step further in that it places literacy within a theoretical framework that acknowledges not only the relational and social context of literacy but also the fact that it is attuned to the imbalances of power influencing literacy development and construction. Using critical literacies is not about shying away from or censoring texts; it is about developing a critical discourse in response to the texts. Acknowledging the positive and pleasurable aspects of media texts does not detract from one's ability to analyze and deconstruct media texts and their meanings. "A balance must emerge so that critical media literacy is not purely a cognitive experience, nor is it solely experiencing pleasures without challenges" (Alvermann, Moon, & Hagood, 1999, p. 28). Schools can be a site where this critical analysis can be taught, shared, and developed.

Having a critical perspective on texts is seen as a necessary step in living an empowered life. For Freire and Macedo (1987), literacy is "[construction of] one's voice as part of a wider project of possibility and empowerment" (p. 7). Literacy is to read the world, that is, to be able to name ones experience and critically situate oneself in the world. "For the notion of literacy to become meaningful," writes Freire (1987), "it has to be situated within a theory of cultural production and viewed as an integral part of the way in which people produce, transform, and reproduce meaning" (p. 142). Reading the world is central to being able to read the word, and both can be used as praxis, that is, "reflection and action upon the world in order to change it" (Freire, 1993, p. 33). In this sense, Freire's view of literacy is very close to bell hooks's (1989) notion of "coming to voice" (p. 54). Both theorists speak to the need for individuals to use texts to form a critical consciousness about themselves and their worlds, including media texts found in the information flood that informs students' lives.

In conclusion, teachers need support to integrate critical media literacy into their existing curriculum. Media literacy as a pedagogical approach has been expanding over the last decade, and sources offer many differing approaches to teaching this topic. There are many different strategies to develop competencies and skills related to media literacy that are outside the scope of this book. However, it is generally agreed that "if media literacy studies are to survive and grow, administrators in schools systems and at individual schools must endorse and support them" (Potter, 2004, p. 245). This study is more evidence for the need to develop critical media literacy skills in middle school classrooms.

CHAPTER 5

Girls, Texts, and Sexualities

One of the themes that dominated the Girls Literacy Discussion Group was sexuality. In fact, topics related to sexuality emerged from the girls every which way I turned. When I asked the girls about their writing in language arts class, they told me they were in the middle of working on persuasive essays. The majority of the girls in the group had chosen abortion as their topic. When I asked about their favorite books, some of the answers were *White Oleander*, a story of an adolescent girl's sexual coming of age; *Am I Blue?*, a collection of stories for and about gay and lesbian youth; and *The House on Mango Street,* whose author describes it as "a book about a young girl's discovery of her sexuality" (Satz, 1997, p. 166).

In one exercise, I asked the girls to write about a character of their choosing from *Seedfolks*, a short novel by Paul Fleishman (1997) that was chosen by the 8th-grade teachers as a book to be read schoolwide for its themes of unity and diversity. Here's what some of them wrote:

> Maricella reminded me of my friend Laquisha. Laquisha was 12 when she had her first kid. She was pregnant in the sixth grade. I really don't think she was old enough to take care of a kid but she did and now her kid is two and she's turning 14. (Kaliya)

> Maricella made me think of my cousin. My cousin was 16 years old when she had her first baby. Her and her boyfriend were really happy 'cause she had a newborn baby. But when my auntie found out, she wanted my cousin to have an abortion 'cause she didn't want her sixteen year old daughter to go through that. But she had it. (Erika)

> My friend Danielle is kind of like Maricella because Maricella is getting judged because she is a pregnant teenager and that's what happened to Danielle. Everybody was judging her, even her own friends. (Moniqua)

> Maricella, she kinds of reminds me of me because she's very blunt about everything. At the beginning she's talking about how if you're

Mexican people don't like you and if you're a pregnant teenager people don't like you and she's says, "I'm a Mexican pregnant 16 year old so shoot me and get over with it." I really liked that because that's something I might say. Well, I won't be a pregnant 16-year-old. I really hope I won't. (Tetra)

Reading their answers, one might come to the conclusion that *Seed-folks* is a book about teen pregnancy, but it is not. The book is only 70 pages long, and only five of those pages refer to Maricella. Yet over half of the girls in the Girls Literacy Discussion Group, independent from one another, chose that character. Readers make meaning and gain knowledge of a text in the interaction between the language on the page and their prior lived experiences and understanding of the world (Rosenblatt, 1994). The girls' focus on the one teen pregnancy in *Seedfolks* provides a window into their lives, their interests, and their "reading of the world." As evidenced by their literacy practices, issues such as teen pregnancy, sexual identity, and sexual expression were prominent in their minds.

Lessons about sexuality and gender are ever-present in both school settings and the out-of-school lives of adolescent girls. Like race and class, sexuality and gender are topics often relegated to the hidden curriculum, which teaches lessons as loudly as a formal educational text. Girls learn about sexuality and gender from the many texts surrounding them. "Girls and young women learn about *doing girl* through multiple contextual cues" (Lloyd, 1998, p. 130). They then use these texts in their construction of their own sexual and gendered selves.

Gender and sexual identity are constructed, in part, by the texts a girl encounters. By examining the texts and contextual cues that girls encounter and the meanings they make of these texts, we can learn more about how they are constructing gender and sexuality for themselves. The texts that the girls mentioned as teaching about sexuality included school lectures, class handouts, church sermons, movies, television shows, music videos, magazines, books, music, advertisements, parent voices, and peer voices. Some texts were regarded as helpful; others, as irrelevant. Some texts elicited a critical analysis; others were accepted without critique. The missing texts, the silences, were also noticeable: texts they wished they had but didn't. Some texts surrounded them and some emerged only occasionally. Overall, the multiple texts from various sources worked together to influence the girls in their meaning-making of themselves, their sense of gender and sexuality in addition to race, class, and culture and where they saw themselves in the world.

When I asked permission from the local school district to conduct this research, I was told, indirectly by the district's Internal Review Board director, to stay away from any conversations about sexuality. This experience reminded me of Michelle Fine's research on high school drop-outs. When she went to speak to the principal of a public high school in New York City about conducting research in his school, his response was, "Sure you can do your research on dropouts at this school with one provision. You cannot mention the words *dropping out* to the students" (Fine & Weis, 2003, p. 18). I would have had just about as much success prohibiting sexuality from the girls' discussions as Fine might have had eliminating dropping out from conversations about leaving school. "The research began with a warning to silence me and the imaginations of these adolescents," Fine wrote. "What became apparent was a systemic fear of naming . . . adults should be so lucky that adolescents wait for us to name the words dropping out or sex for them to do it" (Fine & Weis, 2003, p. 18).

Early in my research I ran into Jennifer Smith in the hallway at Lincoln Middle School. Jennifer was a White Christian conservative teacher in her mid-50s at Lincoln Middle School with whom I had worked years earlier. She asked me what I was doing there, and I told her that I was running a Girls Literacy Discussion Group with some 8th-grade girls. She gave me a forced smile with a puckered look and walked away.

Later that week, Ms. Carpenter, the language arts teacher, whispered to me, "I have something to tell you." We met up later, after class. "I wasn't sure whether to tell you or not, but I thought you'd want to know," she said. She then explained that Jennifer Smith had gone to the principal to warn her about me — that I might be teaching the girls about sexuality, that when I had taught there a few years ago and left on maternity leave, they had found "inappropriate" books in my classroom, like *Our Bodies Ourselves* and *Am I Blue?* and other books about adolescent development. Ms. Carpenter assured me, "I spoke to the principal and told her that I approved everything you gave the girls."

For the next few months I was very careful to watch my back. The research had been approved of by the university, the district, the principal, and the teacher; still, Jennifer Smith weighed on my mind. It is this kind of fear of retribution that acts as a censoring agent in classrooms, resulting in a silencing of "dangerous" topics. Institutional silencing, however, cannot completely control the minds or actions of adolescent girls or prevent their exposure to texts about sexuality and gender.

SCHOOL AND CHURCH TEXTS

The girls mentioned learning about sexuality from both school and church, but both sources were seen as missing the mark when it came to providing information that was relevant, useful, and nonbiased. The girls listed the school sex education classes as spaces where they had learned about sexuality, but they felt that the instruction did not go far enough in providing useful information connected to their real lives. Moniqua, in particular, was a harsh critic:

> You know those little classes in 5th grade, 6th grade? You know how they do that in school? They don't teach you anything you should know. They teach you the abstinence-only education but no one, but no one's going to listen to that. If they want to have sex, they'll go out and they'll do it.

Moniqua, in her comment "they don't teach you anything you should know," indicated her belief that not only is the sex education curriculum irrelevant but the schools are negligent by omitting important information that young people need to have. Abstinence education has become a political position that values "morality" education over giving students information. Abstinence-only education is centered on creating silences, excluding texts and discourses that have an authentic place in the lives of adolescents. If students are to "read" their worlds, then schools need to see the real lives of adolescents.

Tetra also had critical remarks about the sex education curriculum and gender bias. "I remember that they spent way more time on the female body than they did on the male body and that pissed me off. I got mad that they wouldn't spend more time on the guys."

Church was also cited by the girls as a source that tried to teach about sexuality but left out crucial conversations. Four of the girls in the study mentioned attending church: Erika, Angela, Moniqua, and Kaliya. Both Erika and Angela attended church weekly, and both mentioned that their churches addressed sexuality as part of their teachings. However, neither Erika, who attended a small Catholic church in a rural neighborhood, nor Angela, who attended a large church in town, viewed the church-based learning about sexuality as significant in their understandings of their own sexuality.

Erika attended her local Catholic church each Sunday with her grandmother and aunt. There, she would meet up with her boyfriend, who lived in the next town. When I first asked whether they talked about sex at church, she said, "No . . . they talk about love a lot." Then she added that they did talk about waiting until marriage to have sex:

> Like our Father Jose, I'm Catholic and oh God, our priest goes on forever and ever! Because my boyfriend, his mom baptized his

friend's baby and the Father went on and on yelling at the kids that were in church: "You're not supposed to be having sex 'til you're married! And God is watching!" I was like "Oh God" and I put my head down and I started laughing and I got in trouble.

Her story demonstrates a disjuncture between a teenage population and a religious leader trying to control or influence his congregants. Perhaps there is a historical legacy in this example. "Shame and guilt were part of the Church's arsenal of socialization techniques in teaching people what it meant for women to be sexual beings. The Church, as well as Spanish and later Anglo society, convinced men that women had to be protected from the outside or public world—that her primary concern should be the family" (Torres, 2003, p. 27). Whether there is a historical and cultural connection or not, the result is still the same: missing authentic dialogue between adolescents and the adults in their lives.

Like Erika, Angela named going to church as a significant part of her life. In this sense, for both girls, church discourse and written texts were central parts of their literacy practices. Angela identified herself as a Christian and attended a large church in the neighborhood. Her internal sense of spirituality and connection to God was central in her current identity formation process. For example, Angela described the movie *The Passion of Christ* as a text that changed her life:

> The movie that changed my life was the *Passion of Christ* because I saw that and I was put in a whole other perspective. . . . It made my faith stronger. . . . Now when I take the Lord's Supper at Church every Sunday I feel like to need to connect with God.

However, even for Angela, the church was not where she learned her information about sexuality. When I asked whether her church group was teaching about sex or sexuality, she replied, "Actually, right now they're having something about sex. We watch this movie and this guy talks about it, how it's right, how it's wrong, and stuff like that." She then added, "But I don't go to that part." Instead, she said that she learned about birth control and sexuality from her older sister and cousin. "My sister talks to me about it," she explained.

PEER TEXT

Angela's comment that she learned about sexuality from her sister, not from church, was not unusual. In fact, overall, the girls said that they learned more from the people in their lives than from any other text. In a sense, voice, or the voices—the opinions, beliefs, rhetoric, feelings of those close to them—was the most powerful text in their lives. The girls listed the words, actions, and beliefs of people close to them as the texts most influential to them. "Literacy events can be considered moments that include speaking, listening, reading and writing" (Moje, Willes, & Fassio, 2001, p. 194). Friends, mothers, fathers, grandparents, cousins, and sisters were named as sources of influence. The girls believed that the spoken words of influential people in their lives carried much more weight than any other texts they encountered.

"I think other people influence who you are," Moniqua said.

"Yeah," Chris affirmed.

"People you know make much more of an influence," agreed Tetra.

Later, Moniqua elaborated. "I think what other people think matters to me a lot . . . like my friends or people who I like. I think that what they think matters to me a lot."

Another time, I asked the girls to name a book, movie, song, or TV show that had changed their lives. Moniqua returned to the same theme— that for her, other people are the most significant text in her life. "Those things don't really change me. I don't recall those things really affecting my life, like changing it in some way. I think people affect my life more than objects do."

When two sources contradicted each other, the girls turned to their real-life experiences to make meaning of the texts. For example, Erika addressed the issue of parents trying to teach abstinence to their children. Moniqua had just critiqued the abstinence-only curriculum and Erika backed her up:

> I think that, like Moniqua said, a teenager wants to do whatever a
> teenager wants to do. If they want to do it, why don't they just do
> it and you know, and if the parent gets mad, you can't do nothing
> about it because you already been there and you done that, so I don't
> see why parents get mad at it. All I say is at least use protection.
> That's all I got to say! God!

Here, Erika was reading the world around her, which spoke much more loudly than the formal sex education curriculum. Erika was the product of a teen pregnancy, as were Kaliya and Moniqua, which totaled half of our group. In this example, she critiqued the hypocrisy of an adult world teaching abstinence when their lives modeled the opposite. The real-life examples taught much more than a written school-based text did.

The girls indicated that they discussed issues of bodies and sexuality not just in our group but also in conversations with both female and male friends. While much of the literature on boys and girls in school emphasizes the different youth experiences based on gender, these girls crossed gender lines for nonsexualized friendships within their distinct social groups. The girls demonstrated a fluidity of friendship in their discussion of boys and girls learning about bodies and sexuality from one another.

"I talk to guys about their thing, too," Erika said to the group, referring to the male body.

"Me, too," quickly asserted Moniqua.

Sometimes the male friends asked the girls specific questions, seeking to obtain information about female bodies and sexuality. "It's really interesting how guys are really interested in how periods work," Moniqua pointed out.

"Yeah," agreed Erika. "They want to know about it."

"Yeah," echoed Moniqua. "You're just sitting there with a whole bunch of guys and you don't have anything to talk about, they'll start talking about it. They like ask questions. Like, does it hurt?"

Tetra offered another example. "'Is it painful?' I was like, 'Is what painful?' He was like, 'You know, the every month thing!' 'The what?!?' 'You know, when it's your time of the month!' He was just really confused! Like he kept asking me weird questions like, 'How do you make sure that it doesn't get on your clothes or something?'"

"If I push on your stomach, will more come out?" added Moniqua with a laugh. "Guys are so stupid! They ask questions like 'If I push on your stomach, will more come out?' I'll tell you something. I won't mention the name. This is just such a stupid theory. He thinks that if you do crunches, you can't get pregnant! Your abs have nothing to do with your reproductive system! What kind of comment is that?!"

In these cases, the girls had the opportunity to be experts for an inexperienced audience. They were aware of the fact that they knew more than the guys about their bodies, and that information, even if just for a brief moment, gave them a sense of power. These were examples of times when the girls were agents in their own knowledge and power, rather than passive recipients or objects. They were, to use Wolf's (1997) terms, "sexual and cultural creators" rather than "victims of culture and sexuality" (p. xvi).

Although they framed themselves as experts at times, the girls also verbalized their share of misinformation. At one point in the conversation about birth control, Erika asserted that "the pill protects you from STDs." However, the other girls jumped in to correct her, leading to a brief argument. Erika stated that her class told her so. Moniqua asserted, "Well, it's wrong. They're teaching you false things because the pill doesn't do anything to diseases. It just helps prevent pregnancy for like 97.3%."

The use of spaces without adult supervision allowed the girls to co-create meaning with their peers. On the one hand, the vision of boys and girls working together to discover their sexualities can have an aura of puppy-love and sweet innocence right out of a Norman Rockwell painting. However, the lack of clear and accurate information is problematic. If teens can only turn to one another, false and harmful information can be spread without being challenged. Furthermore, without adult support, adolescents are left to navigate such important arenas on their own, sometimes resulting in risky choices.

MOTHER TEXT

Mothers were a significant topic to the girls in the group. The messages from their mothers, what I am calling "mother text," were important texts in their lives. Overall, the girls felt that the connections with their mother were incredibly significant in their lives, their learning, and their sense of self. In contrast of mainstream media images, which present the typical adolescent girl as at odds with her mother, many of the girls in this study indicated that they felt strongly connected with their mothers and that they could talk to them about anything, including sexuality. Others discussed the pain of wanting to connect more deeply with their mothers but not knowing how.

"I think that we need love and without love from someone that's so big and important in our lives that can really screw you over," pondered Tetra. "If my mom started to ignore me, I'd feel so sad. I tell my mom everything. I'd have a mental breakdown, and go insane."

Kaliya concurred. "That's what I like," Kaliya explained. "I can connect with my mom. I didn't used to think that I could. I didn't tell my mom anything, and then she came to me, and she was like, 'If you ever need something, and you need to tell me about it, you can talk to me about it.'"

Later, during a conversation about sexuality and learning about sex, Tetra said, "My mom just wants me to know everything I can. She's always like, if you ever want to talk about anything, come talk to me."

Moniqua questioned Tetra. "You can't talk to your mom!"

"I can," asserted Tetra. "It's awesome!"

Tetra continued with her story. "I can tell my mom, 'How does this or that work?' 'Well, if you consult the manual.' Poom! My mom actually gave me a book this thick about reproductive organs on males and females specifically made to entertain a teen, and it talks about pelvic exams and how to make sure you don't get infections and everything. Every time I have a question, my mom pulls out that book." Again, with Tetra, we see how the extensive family literacy supported here in her development of self. Tetra made another reference to her mother's literacy practices. The girls were talking about menstruation, and Tetra informed the other girls about a kind of diaphragm that can be used to hold menstrual blood. "I saw it in [my mom's] *Bitch* magazine and I thought it was really funny . . . so my mom bought me a little packet of those things. They seemed really neat."

In some ways, Erika's mother was similar to Tetra's in providing her daughter with information and resources to support her emerging sexuality. When the girls were discussing pelvic exams, Moniqua was inquisitive and frightened, but Erika said, "My mom gave me the details. I guess she had to get one of those. She was like, 'Yeah, I had to put my legs like this.'"

On another day, we read excerpts from *The Body Project: An Intimate History of American Girls* (Brumberg, 1997). The girls brought the conversation around to issues of sexuality and birth control. Erika was offering a lot of information on the topic; when I asked her where she had learned so much, she said that her mother had signed her up for a sex education class at her local public health clinic.

"My mom took me to school for it," Erika explained. "She put me in a program because she thinks that I am going to go and have sex with guys. My mom's stupid."

Erika described the class, "There were at least fifteen girls there. . . . They talk about different [birth control] you could get." Although she told the other girls "My mom's stupid" for signing her up for the course, I could sense an underlying satisfaction and pride in both taking the class and her connection with her mother.

Although her mother provided her with this information and support, Erika still said that it was hard for her to talk with her mother about sex and sexuality. "I can't talk to my mom. I don't like talking to her. I have to tell a friend. I can't just go up to my mom and say 'Hey, Mom! Guess what? Here's how I have sex!' I can't just tell her that!"

When I asked if her mother talked with her about sex, she answered, "Yeah, but then I walk away 'cause I don't want to hear about it! They talk on forever and ever, especially if she's around my nana and auntie! Oh God!" she added with an exasperated sigh.

"If you're going to do something, tell me so I can go get you on something!" Erika mimicked. "They want to know all about it. . . . My mom wants me to go out and tell her. If I have sex or something, she'll want to me to tell her. Who? Who was he? Everything. Where? What time? Everything. Did you use a condom? Ugh!" These conversations occurred in the group discussions, with other girls as an active audience, so it was hard to tell if she was performing a certain identity that separated her from her mother, particularly to align herself with Moniqua, one that might have been differently enacted if Erika was speaking to me alone.

In contrast to Tetra and Kaliya, Moniqua, out of all the girls, often expressed a desire for authentic dialogue about sexuality and womanhood with her mother but felt that she was met with silence. "I can barely live with her!" Moniqua said about her mother.

When Erika was talking about her mother wanting to discuss sex, Moniqua interjected with intensity, "At least your mom talks to you about it. Instead of ignoring it!"

When I later asked Moniqua where she had learned about birth control, she responded, "Like I remember in 5th grade we talked a lot about it because we had a class." She continued, "We talked about it a lot. Not me and my mom. Oh no, my mom completely walks out of the subject."

Angela echoed this response as well. She learned about birth control and sexuality from her sister and her cousin. "My mom, she doesn't talk about it."

Moniqua elaborated. "Neither does my mom," she affirmed to Angela. "My mom, she's probably like your mom. She completely blocks out the issue. Like if she knows something and doesn't want to talk about it, she just lets it go. She pretends she doesn't know anything, pretends it doesn't exist."

In this group, the mother-daughter interactions were powerful texts that girls "read" to make sense of themselves and their worlds. Both the spoken words and the silences were given meaning and significance by the girls. Mothers, like their daughters, are also constantly interacting with texts and creating their sense of self, including what it means to be a mother. As they perform motherhood, they are also exploring what they believe is appropriate to talk about with an adolescent daughter and what is not. They, too, are interacting with texts, cultural norms, class values, and personal histories to form their own sense of being a mother. The dance between the positioning of daughter to mother and mother to daughter forms the texts that co-create their connection to each other.

TEXTS THAT POLICE AND MONITOR GIRLS' BEHAVIOR AND CLOTHES

One of the most significant ways in which parents, both mothers and fathers, discuss matters of sexuality and their bodies with their daughters is around issues of monitoring them to try to keep them safe and protected. This theme, of being monitored by parents, came up over and over again. The girls discussed at length how their mothers and fathers tried to control and police their movement and activities, clothes and appearances. "My mom won't let me go to the movies with my boyfriend," Erika complained to me in our first individual interview. "She won't, because she's protecting me. I hate that! Then he wants to go take pictures with me at the image shots at the mall, and she won't let me go. She'll only let me see him at church or when I'm with my parents. Like if we want to be by ourselves, we'll go to the back of my nana's and sit on the swing."

For Erika, who mentioned more restrictions than the other girls, the protectionist stance, or "cloistering and sexual policing," may be related to her Chicana culture (Lopez, 2003, p. 121). "Young women in Chicano/ Mexicano communities are closely monitored by their parents, their mothers in particular, until they are handed over to their next 'keeper,' ideally a husband. . . . A major motive for women's restriction is the preservation of their virginity until marriage" (Hurtado, 2003, p. 38). The messages Erika received in her Hispanic Catholic church resonated with this perspective.

While the extent or reasons may or may not be culturally related, the experience of adolescent girls being controlled or sexually policed crosses race, class, and culture lines. Adolescence, a time when young people individuate from their parents and yearn to explore new worlds separate from those of their parents, is the same time that most adolescent girls in our society are physically reined in by parents as an effort to protect them from sexual violence or sexual activities. "The young girl's lust for space comes at the same moment her culture tells her that her developing body puts her in danger whenever she roams 'too far'"(Wolf, 1997, p. 29). These conflicting narratives created tension for the girls.

In addition to being monitored in the physical realm, both Erika and Tetra described being monitored on the Internet. Erika shared this experience about her boyfriend: "His mom makes fun of him when I e-mail him. Because when he gets it, his mom's right by him reading it."

Similarly, Tetra found that when she searched on the Internet for information about sexual identity, her father watched over her shoulder:

My dad is slightly homophobic, which is kind of creepy, so mainly I don't go to those sites because my dad, every time he passes by, he has to look over your shoulder and see what you're doing and you're like, "Dad, what if I was writing down my deepest, darkest secret and I didn't want anyone to see it. And you keep looking over my shoulder, and you're reading my secret!" He does that. [*Sigh*] I just want to kill him when he does it.

In all of these cases, parents were trying to keep their children safe. It is a reality that adolescent girls can be targets of violence. The media presents many images of the vulnerability of adolescent girls in particular.

However, while parents' intentions are to protect their daughters from harm, an underlying problematic message can be conveyed by this protective stance: that girls' bodies are both dangerous and vulnerable and, therefore, need to be controlled and protected. This framing of adolescent girls' sexualities and bodies, with an "insistence on defining female adolescent sexuality only in terms of disease, victimization and morality," results in an "avoidance of girls' own feelings of sexual desire and pleasure" as well as a silenced conversation of such topics central to girls' lives (Tolman, 2005, p. 14). The girls expressed resentment toward parents who monitored and policed their bodies, actions, clothes, and makeup. When I asked if they felt there was a real risk of sexual assault, the girls ignored the question and continued to complain about what they saw as overprotective parents.

Often the symbol of protection/policing was clothing. Over and over, the girls discussed arguments with their parents about "inappropriate" clothing. Here's an example from Moniqua: "I was going out and all of a sudden my mom decided what I was wearing was 'inappropriate' because it was cut low," Moniqua told the group. "So I just listened to her talking the whole way to the mall, and she keeps talking about, 'Well, don't get raped. Don't get raped.'"

Kaliya gave her own example. "My dad's overprotective," she complained. "Because we went to Fun Park and there's these fine guys, you know." She laughed. "And I'm staring at them and I'm wearing a bathing suit and my dad's like 'Go put a T-shirt on' and I was like 'Why?' 'Because it's just inappropriate.' And it was a *bathing suit!*" Kaliya demonstrated desire by looking at boys she found attractive and by pausing and letting them look at her in a bathing suit. Her father stepped into the situation and attempted to control, or eliminate, her sexual expression by controlling her outfit. Whether he believed that she was at risk of sexual assault or whether he was uncomfortable with her asserting her sexual desire was unclear, but either way, his behavior served to curtail both.

The term *inappropriate* came up many times as a blanket term to suppress girls' sexual expressions. After Kaliya told her story, Moniqua pointed out, "But it wasn't 'inappropriate' until you saw them [the boys]!" Moniqua swiftly centered on the key issue: that it wasn't the clothing but the sexual desire that was deemed "inappropriate." Over and over, the girls gave examples where clothing became "inappropriate" in a context where it was linked with desire. Moniqua explained, "My mom tells what's appropriate and what's not. If I wear something that's inappropriate, she always gives me this face that says, 'that's not appropriate.'"

Tetra noted that even strangers use the term *inappropriate* to control the sexuality or sexual expression of girls they don't even know, a form of "external surveillance" (Fine, 1992, p. 185). Tetra explained:

Even people on the street do that. I've noticed that my cousin, she's the tight-pants, tube-top woman of the world, and when she goes out, her parents will tell her "don't do it," but sometimes just random people we don't even know, women on the street that we don't know, will come up and tell her, "That's inappropriate dress wear for out on the street!"

Underneath these adult-teenager scripts is the issue of control. "One of the main areas of contention that arise between parents or adult authority figures and adolescents centers on exactly this question: who has the right to control this body? . . . Who owns the body? Who is responsible for this body and its actions?" (Bloustien, 2004, p. 69). The parents were trying to control their daughters' bodies, in an effort to protect them, and the girls were struggling to become active agents in their own decisions and life choices. If the body is a text, this struggle for control is parallel to the struggles of finding one's voice and reading one's world.

Here Erika struggled with her mother to "voice" her sexual desire:

That's what my mom tells me! [My mom says] "Go put on your suit!" "It don't fit me no more!" That was when I was 12. My mom got all mad 'cause we were at the Fun Park and I saw some guys and they were all whistling at me. I put my head down and then I went to go talk to them and my mom was all "Get your ass over here!" And I was all "Why?" She's all "Go put on a fucking shirt!" I was all "God!"

Again, the girl was chastised for showing desire or interest in boys. When I asked if they thought their parents were controlling them because they didn't want them showing sexual interest in boys, or if they thought their parents were afraid of sexual assault, they indicated that both were a factor. Kaliya provided an example of when her mother tried to protect her from what her mother believed to be a sexual predator.

One time we were at Walmart and this guy, he's like old, like 20-something, and he was like "Oooooo baby!" and my mom screamed "SHE'S 13. DON'T BE TALKING TO MY DAUGHTER LIKE THAT!" And I was wearing a wife-beater (tank top) and I had it tied in the back and it was showing my stomach and my mom was like "Kaliya, zip up that jacket!" and then she's all yelling, "DON'T YOU LOOK AT MY DAUGHTER! KEEP WALKING! KEEP WALKING!"

The girls were not only frustrated at being controlled; they were often enraged by what they saw as a double standard in expectations of shrouding one's body between themselves and their brothers, between adolescent girls and boys. "They can go without a shirt and they don't care!" exclaimed Moniqua.

"And they can wear baggy pants," added Kaliya.

"Showing their butt! They don't get in trouble, but what is up with the girls!?!" declared Erika.

"Guys get away with everything, that's what I don't get. Guys get away with everything. They can wear whatever they want, but say me, Kaliya, and Moniqua went out and we're wearing tight pants with a small shirt. We get yelled at 'cause we're showing a little. I like to show my stomach a little! Not where everybody can see everything!"

"OK, if you're wearing a shirt and showing your stomach a little you get yelled at, but guys can walk around with their shirts off!" Moniqua pointed out.

For Kaliya, who had a teenage brother, the injustice hit home. "You'll be wearing something that's close-covering, like I was wearing these pants and they weren't tight to me but I guess they looked tight and my dad was like, 'Why are you wearing those tight pants?!' And I was like, 'Why is Daren wearing baggy pants?!' I'm like, 'At least I'm covering something. Daren's showing his crack and all!!'"

We see the girls here using critical literacy skills to observe and critique the injustices that they see in their worlds. In many examples, they are bumping up against parents who send them both liberating and stifling messages at the same time. Feminist theorist Uma Narayan (1997) speaks to this contradiction: "Both our mothers and our mother-cultures give us all sorts of contradictory messages, encouraging their daughters to be confident, impudent and self-assertive even as they attempt to instill conformity, decorum and silence, seemingly oblivious to these contradictions" (p. 8). These contradictory messages are an indication of the complexity of the human experience, where we parents, like our daughters, perform different and sometimes contradictory perspectives in a complex and multifaceted world.

IMPLICATIONS AND RECOMMENDATIONS

I found over and over that the girls wanted to talk, read, and write about gender and sexuality. This topic was a missing discourse in their lives. "What I'm thinking," posed Moniqua. "Why don't they just give us the information because we're going to do whatever we want anyways; we might as well be educated about it and not go and be stupid."

The girls in my research wanted access to the correct information. They wanted someone to talk openly with them, answer their questions, and fill in the gaps. Likewise, Tolman (2005), in her study of adolescent girls and sexuality, found that her participants also searched for ways to have conversations with their mothers and other adult women about sexuality. When asked, they advised adults to give them opportunities to explore and discuss how they experience themselves as sexual beings. Tolman noted that "whether out of fear for their children or their own discomfort with sexuality, the ways in which adults do speak to adolescents about sexuality are (often) impoverished" (2005, p. 202). Girls are left lacking information they seek on their journey of understanding themselves and the worlds around them.

The girls indicated that there was room for parents and educators to step into teachable moments by embracing the opening and engaging in an honest and authentic conversation about their lives, perspectives, and experiences. The gaps point to the need for a "genuine discourse of desire" and sexuality and gender, one that "would invite adolescents to explore what feels good and bad, desirable and undesirable, grounded in experience, needs and limits . . . a discourse that would pose female adolescents as subjects of [their] sexuality" (Fine & Weis, 2003, p. 43). This discourse would in turn add to the existing texts that girls engage with as they construct themselves as young women.

As mothers, as parents, who want to raise girls who are strong and powerful and empowered, we need to figure out how to have open dialogue with our daughters that addresses the struggle to have a free and open sexuality coupled with the reality that sometimes ours is not a safe world for girls. We need to have conversations that address this challenge that all women face: navigating the world safely while pushing for our freedom of expression. We need to find ways to address the complexities of whom do we want to be attractive for, and whom do we want to be sexual with, and why do we want to be sexual, and when does it make sense to be sexual, and how do we be sexual beings but also make sure that we are holding onto our self-esteem and our personal power. Our daughters are coming of age in a culture that is hypersexualized even as it forbids in-depth, inquiry-based sex education. As mothers, we can be one of the texts that make a difference in their lives, that teaches the fragile balance of protection and empowerment.

In this school district, teachers are strongly discouraged from discussing sexuality in the classroom, and teachers feel this pressure to avoid such controversial topics. In one classroom observation, Ms. Carpenter was teaching a unit on poetry; when one of the poems had a subtle sexual reference, she referred to it as "the birds and the bees" and then said, "wink, wink." There was clearly no room in that classroom for Erika to share her expertise about birth control methods or for Tetra to discuss her emerging bisexual/lesbian identity.

Teachers must be allowed, encouraged, and expected to include sexuality in the middle school curriculum in a meaningful and authentic way. As indicated in my research, sexual identity, sexual performance, sexual stereotypes, relationships, pregnancy, and sexual protection are key issues for adolescent girls. Silencing such conversations and ignoring such topics not only create dissonance between the classroom curriculum and students' real lives but also create a missed opportunity for learning. The current educational focus on abstinence to the exclusion of all else not only fosters denial and disengagement but is also dangerous for our youth. As Fine (1992) wrote:

> In order to understand the sexual subjectivities of young women more completely, educators need to reconstruct schooling as an empowering context in which we listen to and work with the meanings and experiences of gender and sexuality revealed by the adolescents themselves. When we refuse that responsibility, we prohibit an education that adolescents wholly need and deserve. (p. 40)

For example, Tetra liked to read books with gay and lesbian characters, listen to lesbian music, and use the Internet to research sexuality, access lesbian Internet sites, and find out about queer youth culture. She found all of these texts outside of the school setting, many of them provided by her mother. These texts helped support Tetra in her coming-out journey. The inclusion of LGBT literature in the schools has long been framed as risk reduction. As one librarian noted, "One of the things we do as librarians is to help kids over the hard times in their lives. If we can give them books that make their world easier to understand, or more palatable, then we've done our jobs" (Woog, 1995, p. 318). Current research on queer youth in school compels us to not only include LGBTQ texts but foster dialogue around issues of heterosexism and homophobia throughout the school year. "If [LGBT-themed] literature were engaged over time, students would be challenged repeatedly to consider what it means for them to be LGBTQ, allied or homophobic" (Clark & Blackburn, 2009, p. 29). This inclusion could change the lives of many middle school students.

For Erika, teen pregnancy was an everyday issue. Erika indicated that she was sexually active with her boyfriend. She also stated that for religious reasons she was opposed to abortion except in cases of rape. Furthermore, her knowledge of contraception was flawed. For example, she thought that the birth control pill also prevented transmission of the HIV virus. This triangle of sexual activity, an anti-abortion stance, and faulty information about birth control made a future teen pregnancy highly possible, if not inevitable. Studies show that if they do not use contraceptives, sexually active teens have a 90% chance of becoming pregnant (Alan

Guttmacher Institute, 2011). Erika had friends who were teen mothers, her closest cousin was a teen mother, and her mother had been a teen mother. Therefore, it made sense that sexuality and pregnancy were issues that Erika wanted to discuss as she made meaning of herself and her world. She needed texts, both fiction and nonfiction, that could give extended meaning to this area of exploration in her life. These were the texts that would pull Erika in and compel her to develop her literacy by actively engaging her, both as a reader and a learner. In Chapter 9, I present the girls' views on teen pregnancy, a topic that repeated itself many times during the course of the research. Teen pregnancy had real-life implications for the girls' futures, their socioeconomic status, and their success in school.

For educators to shy away from such topics is not only pedagogically unsound but also simply irresponsible. The state where this research took place has one of the highest teen birth rates in the United States. In the Lincoln Middle School district, 48% of the high school students reported being sexually active and 45% of those reported not using a condom during the last sexual intercourse. In addition, the state's chlamydia rate is nearly 50% higher than the U.S. rate and even higher in this city and currently rising among the teen population. Clearly, sex education is a public health issue in addition to an area of concern for educators.

Since sexuality is a significant theme and issue in the lives of many urban adolescent girls, it should be integrated into the curriculum. At times, Ms. Carpenter did this in her teaching. For example, she included books in the curriculum that had themes of sexuality, such as *The House on Mango Street.* Similarly, when it came to independent reading, Ms. Carpenter encouraged students to choose their own books and made books available to them that she thought they might enjoy, including books that dealt with gay-and-lesbian issues as well as other issues of sexuality. She gave broad and open writing assignments, such as choose a person you admire or write about a controversial topic of your choice, which allowed the girls to choose topics like abortion and teen pregnancy. Even Erika, who rarely turned work in, wrote and handed in an essay about abortion.

Classrooms must be spaces where the voices and experiences of all students are honored, valued, and heard. Real-life issues such as teen pregnancy, birth control, and sexual orientation need a place in the middle school curriculum. A curriculum that is muddied by silences and taboos and that is dominated by hegemonic culture and values to the exclusion of all else will result in uninterested and disengaged students. Students who have less invested, less social capital, and less connection to the White middle-class culture are more likely to become disengaged.

Teachers are afraid of broaching topics like sexuality. They fear for their jobs, they fear that they don't have the skills and/or training to cover such topics, or they fear retribution from parents or administrators. It seems easier to delegate such topics to the PE teacher, the coaches, the health education teacher, or the counselor. When I taught education methods classes to student teachers in a college of education program, I found that often what blocked conversations about sexuality was fear, often based on cultural values that promoted silencing around certain topics.

There are challenges in creating access to these kinds of texts. As educators, we often run into protectionist and reactionary perspectives toward children and curricula. Teachers who are out there taking risks fear retribution from the "Jennifer Smiths" who want to silence conversations around "dangerous" topics.

As a middle school teacher myself, I found one strategy that helped me reduce my fear of reprimand from parents or administrators. In my middle school language arts classroom, I had a large library of many different kinds of books and often assigned independent reading projects that allowed students to pick books of their level, interest, and focus area. I taught the students how to assess whether a book was or was not at their level, what to do if the content made them uncomfortable, and how to pick a good book to read. At the beginning of the school year, I sent home contracts to parents explaining that I had an open classroom library and that it was the parents' job to discuss with their children what they were reading and supervise their decision-making process. This policy helped protect me from parental or administrative complaints at the same time that it allowed parents to have a relationship with their children regarding choice of reading materials. Over the years, I never had any complaints from parents about this policy or any of the books in my classroom library.

Allowing for authentic empowerment is a messy and risky business. However, we must take these risks and overcome the barriers to make room for authentic learning for our students. As teachers, we must be willing to be agents for change in order to inspire our students to do the same.

CHAPTER 6

Reading Violence in Their Worlds

For many middle school girls across the United States, violence is an everyday reality in their lives. According to the U.S. Department of Justice (2007), 59% of households experiencing reported incidences of domestic violence (intimate partner violence) had children as part of the household. Family violence accounted for 1 in 10 violent victimizations and three-fourths of these occurred near or in the family residence with the majority of victims were female (Bureau of Justice Statistics, 2005). For the members of the Girls Literacy Discussion Group, violence was a text with which they interacted and therefore read and had to make meaning of. Unfortunately, open discussions of violence are often seen as taboo in the public school classroom and are relegated to the hidden curriculum that permeates middle school girls' experiences.

VIOLENCE AS A TEXT

Violence was a significant text in Erika's life. Her father was a local gang leader who had been in and out of prison. In personal writing and individual interviews, Erika described incidents of domestic violence, gang shootings in her neighborhood, and her own suspensions for fighting as well as those of her boyfriend. In her world, violence was a text that Erika had a transactional relationship with as she sought to understand it, her relationship to it, and what it could teach her about herself in the world.

After one of our first Girls Literacy Discussion Group meetings, Erika lingered behind. She had something to tell me and waited for the other girls to leave. "My mom's husband left," she told me. We talked for a few minutes, and I sensed the weight of the stress she was experiencing. I asked her if she had told her teacher.

"I can't talk to her," she responded with her head down, eyes averted.

I asked her if I could talk to the teacher for her, and she agreed. She returned to class and later I met with Ms. Carpenter, who related that she had been worried about Erika and wondered if she was a victim of physical and/or sexual abuse because of the way she behaved in class, often

withdrawn and at other times easily drawn into physical fights and conflict. Ms. Carpenter told me she planned to speak to the school counselor
and to Erika herself the next time she had a chance.

The conflict between Erika's mother and husband lasted throughout
the semester, with the husband moving in and out of the house several
times. Every so often, Erika gave me updates. In her second individual
interview, we sat together in a corner of the empty school library and she
told me more of the family history:

> When I was 5, that's when my mom left my dad because my dad
> was hitting my mom all the time and he didn't take care of me. . . .
> When I was 6, my brother was born. And my mom had my brother
> from a different dad. Then his dad used to beat my mom a lot, and
> my mom stayed with him still but was cheating on him at the same
> time. . . . My brother's dad keeps on going to the house and wants to
> see my brother, and then my brother cries because he can't see him.

While the family struggled with conflict and crisis, Erika helped to
support her mother and the family through the chaos. Erika described the
situation to me: "It's kind of bad because my mom's like lost now that she
don't have him [the husband] and she's going through a hard time. I'm
going through a hard time, too, because I gotta keep her standing up tall."
Erika's emotional support of her mother is not uncommon for girls, particularly girls in low-income families. In her study on poor women and girls,
Dodson (1999) found that the girls often described "filling a role of media-
tion, advocacy and caretaking in a family in which the adult strength has
broken down" (p. 29). Dodson noted that "this disintegration comes about
in various ways, but the most common stories concern domestic violence,
parental substance abuse, or when a mother becomes physically or men-
tally unable to perform" (p. 29). This role may be amplified for Latina/
Hispanic girls like Erika (Denner & Guzman, 2006).

While families with economic resources have a variety of social and
medical services available to them, low-income families have much less
access to such supports. Therefore, "the external disadvantages faced by
low-income families coupled with the demands of raising children without money, often alone, exaggerate the demands placed upon low-income
parents" (Dodson, 1999, p. 8). As more demands are placed on parents,
these demands, in turn, are placed on their children and, in greater force,
on teenage daughters. In national data, low-income students drop out
at a higher rate than other youth. Girls are much more likely to name
family concerns as the primary cause of leaving school. For Latina drop-
outs, family responsibilities are their most likely stated reason for leaving

school (Stearns & Glennie, 2006, p. 45). The work these girls do to hold their families together is often invisible to teachers, administrators, and the larger society. "Alongside over-worked parents, invisible girls take care of family life in poor America and they do so at no small cost to themselves" (Dodson, 1999, p. 49). Erika's family work and the toll it took on her was, for the most part, invisible to the school system.

In addition to helping her mother cope with a life of domestic violence and difficulty, Erika also struggled with her own relationship to violence and her own emotional scars and wounds. On several occasions, she gave indications of violence she had faced, although she never went into detail in her conversations with me. For example, about her "real dad" she said, "Last time I seen him, I was hurt because me and him used to tell everything and he pushed me away. I was going to give him a hug. When I seen him, he pushed me away. I just, whatever, left." She used the same language, the term, *pushed*, to refer to her mother's husband. When I asked why she didn't call him her stepfather, she vigorously shook her head "no" and said, "We don't like each other." She then told me this anecdote:

> When he came home, we got mad at each other because he said that the house wasn't clean, but it was. There was just a little mess on the floor because my brother was making a mess. He got mad, and I started copping an attitude with him, and he copped one back with me. Then he pushed me and I was like, "Don't push me!" I started crying, and he kept on pushing me, and I started cussing at him. I didn't mean to.

It was clear to me by the way she consistently brought the topic up in whatever private moment she had with me that the family conflicts weighed heavily on her and were central in her world. The grief Erika held was ever-present, and she seemed to be waiting for openings to express herself. In a writing activity, the members of the Girls Literacy Discussion Group wrote about a difficulty they had faced in the past and what had helped them overcome the obstacle. (See Figure 6.1.)

Erika herself struggled with her own personal relationship with violence. She had already been suspended for fighting and was moved out of her last school for the same reason. "My mom just wanted me to come to a school over here because I got into too much fights over there and I got into a bunch of fights with my teachers and the principal." About her boyfriend she said, "He's like me. He gets into a bunch of fights and stuff." She worried about him, saying, "He can't get in any more fights because if he does, he's going to jail, and I don't want him to go to jail."

Another topic that Erika spoke about at length in her individual interviews was her family's involvement with a local gang. Both through

Figure 6.1. Erika's Hard Time

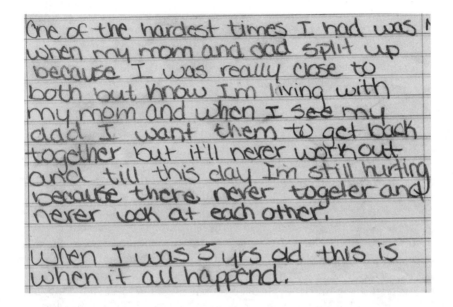

One of the hardest times I had was when my mom and dad split up because I was really close to both but now I'm living with my mom and when I see my dad I want them to get back together but it'll never work out and till this day I'm still hurting because they're never together and never look at each other. When I was 5 years old this is when it all happened.

firsthand experience and via family oral history, Erika had extensive knowledge of the players, history, and politics of her father's gang and its interactions with a rival gang. According to Erika, these two gangs had been warring for years, and a current conflict had brought increased tension and violence to her community. For example, Erika explained, "Now there's a bunch of shootings in [my part of town]. One's by my grandma's house, right next door to her, and there's been a lot. Then they put 'Red Rum' on everybody's car and everything. They spelled 'Red Rum.' It means 'Murder' backwards."

Erika was worried about her father, who was a gang leader and had previously been in prison: "[The gang wars] scare me because my dad's in it because I don't want to get a phone call saying that my dad is dead." Erika lived in the gang war zone and worried for her own safety: "We live on the other side of [town]. . . across the train tracks, and our house is right here, and there's another house [next door] where a bunch of gang bangers go. . . . I know them. They won't do nothing. But let's say if the people from California came driving by my house, they'd shoot each other." She had been raised in this environment and had witnessed violence both in her home and in the street. About the gang she said:

> People like being in a gang because it gets them money from selling drugs on the street and doing a bunch of stuff. I know what they do, but it's like really violent because I seen it happen. Like I seen Down Town go to war with another side while another side goes to war with each other and oh God, you don't want to see that.

When speaking about the gangs, Erika described how her father and neighbors and "all the guys I used to hang out with" were involved with the gangs, but Erika asserted several times that she was not personally "in" the gang. She said, "My friend Jose, Michael, Ernie, Gabe, all of them are in there. All the guys I used to hang out with. They're all in that gang but they're stupid." She also said that if she were to be in a gang, she'd be in Down Town Gang "because I know a lot of people from there and we're like really, really close." Then she told me, "[My father] wants me to be involved in [the gang], too. He asked me if I wanted to be in a gang, and I told him 'no.'" Erika later went on to say, "I wouldn't want to get into it because like, you'll have to do certain things to get into it and I don't want to do that and I don't want to hurt my family like other people do when they get into gangs. Shooting people, getting killed, or nothing like that."

In her discussion about her family's gang culture, Erika demonstrated significant literacies, both in terms of her own understanding of her world and her absorption of a family and cultural oral history. Erika was able to explain to me the complex interpersonal and political dynamics of the situation as well as translate some of the terms and their significance, as indicated in the "Red Rum" example above. I was an outsider to this gang culture; yet Erika quite adeptly painted a picture that allowed me, for a moment, to enter that piece of her world.

During the course of the semester, these gangs were highlighted on the local news. Erika discussed her family's involvement with the gangs only during individual interviews, not during language arts class or the Girls Literacy Discussion Group. The only time Erika mentioned the gangs in the group was when her dad's friend, who was wanted for murder, was shown on the evening news. While the other girls mentioned television shows frequently, this reference was also only the second time that Erika had ever referred to television; the first time she parroted that her favorite show was *Friends*. On this latter occasion, Erika became the star of the group as she captivated the other girls with a tale of a fugitive on the loose. However, the attention lasted less than a few minutes as the other girls switched the topic to something else.

Due to the stigmatization of gang culture in the larger schooling context, there was no space in the classroom or the school culture for Erika to share her expertise regarding this significant part of her life. Although Erika had mentioned the gangs to me on several occasions, when I asked Ms. Carpenter, she indicated that she had no knowledge of Erika's or her family's connection to gangs. These silences led to a lost opportunity, for both Erika and the school, to engage in real dialogue and learning from one another in this area.

When the language arts teacher learned of Erika's family difficulties, her response was to refer Erika to the school counselor. At Lincoln Middle School, there were two school counselors for over 800 students. Both counselors were women; one was White and the other was Latina. While I support the efforts of the teacher to get emotional help for Erika during this difficult period, I also agree with Michelle Fine, who asserted that the silencing around issues of violence, poverty, and family conflict in the classroom and the relegation of those subjects exclusively to school counselors reinforces a class-based institutionalized silence in the classroom. Fine found that "the lived experiences of all adolescents, and particularly those surviving city life in poverty, place their physical and mental well-being as well as that of their kin in constant jeopardy" (Fine & Weis, 2003, p. 28). And yet, in schools across the United States, "conversations about these very conditions of life, about alcoholism, drug abuse, domestic violence, environmental hazards, gentrification and poor health—to the extent that they all happened at all—remained confined to individual sessions with counselors" (p. 28). This "privatizing and psychologizing of public and political issues serves to reinforce the alienation of students' lives from their educational experience" (p. 29). For a girl like Erika, by being sent to a counselor to talk about these central issues, the message she retains may be that there is no room for such topics in the classroom learning environment.

Because her knowledge, experience, and interest base were deemed "unacceptable" by the formal school culture, Erika's expression of literacies within the school walls was stifled if not stigmatized. Her life, which centered on her boyfriend, sexuality, gang politics, family conflict, religious practices, popular culture, and Hispanic familial and cultural events, was nearly invisible within the literacy of formal schooling. Erika remained silent in the classroom not because she was shy but because there was no room for what she had to say.

Likewise, Moje, Willes, and Fassio's (2001), in their study of 7th graders, found that one of their participants, Chile, "told [the researcher] a number of stories about gang practices and was according to the assistant principal, 'deeply involved' with gangs [but] she never wrote about gang activity" (p. 204). The researchers noted, "It is hardly surprising that Chile resisted writing about gangs" (p. 204). Gang activity, after all, was heavily prohibited by the school, and her "failure to write about something so predominant in her life and her focus on acceptable topics reveals an additional flaw in expressivist writing pedagogies: Few students will choose to write about their authentic experiences if those experiences are not sanctioned in school and classroom cultures" (p. 205). Similarly, Erika's experiences with gang culture were silenced and never entered the classroom.

Making room for voices, literacies, and lived experiences like Erika's would be a first step in breaking down the hegemonic privileging of White middle-class voices and shifting schools to be successful learning spaces for all students. As Michelle Fine noted, "What if these voices, along with the chorus of drop-outs, were allowed expression? What if they were not whispered, isolated or drowned out in disparagement, what would happen if these stories were solicited, celebrated and woven into a curriculum?" (Fine & Weis, 2003, p. 33) I myself wondered: What if Erika's voice were to ring out in the classroom as it does in the hallways?

IMPLICATIONS AND RECOMMENDATIONS

Disengaged students are ones who are disconnected from the classroom culture and conversations. Middle school teachers can keep students engaged in the curriculum and learning by making links between their worlds outside of school and the world inside the classroom. As educator Lisa Delpit (2002) wrote:

> If we are to invite children into the language of school, we must make school inviting to them. In almost every school I have visited, private conversations with children will elicit the same response: Almost no one in the school ever listens to them. There is no more certain way to insure that people do not listen to you as to not listen to them. Furthermore, by not listening, teacher cannot know what students are concerned about, what interests them, or what is happening in their lives. Without that knowledge, it is difficult to connect the curriculum to anything students find meaningful. (p. 42)

All middle school classrooms should integrate skill-building with a focus on the development of adolescents as a whole, including an integration of their interests and backgrounds. As Bruya and Olwell (2006) explained, "The most powerful learning in schools is often found in activities that harness individual students' interests and creativity . . . also found in activities that connect directly to the world around the students" (p. 31). Such scaffolding would especially support the achievement of second-language learners, previously disengaged and marginalized students, as well as the rest of the student body. Students like Erika could benefit from a classroom where they are truly seen, with all of their difficult life events, strengths, struggles, and desires. This strategy would include in the classroom texts that address key issues like race, class, sexuality, and violence because these are the issues that are not only in our students lives but are culturally and age appropriate for adolescents.

Many middle school teachers have embraced the recommendation of incorporating into the curriculum culturally diverse texts or "culturally relevent" texts, to use the term Ladson-Billings (1995) coined. Ms. Carpenter, the language arts teacher, was implementing this strategy in her classroom. Students were often given choices of novels to read, both for ailent sustained reading time and literature book groups. Aware of the diversity of her students, the teacher made sure that the selection of books represented an array of races, cultures, and male and female protagonists. The students in my research noted that they were appreciative of the teacher's efforts in this area, and they often actively chose books that contained characters of their own race and culture.

The next step in diversifying texts would be to include texts that represent diverse experiences, including those that address issues of sexuality, sexual orientation, violence, and conflict, which I consider age appropriate. *Age-appropriate* is a term often used to keep teachers from exposing children to texts that are beyond their knowledge or understanding. In this case, I am pushing in the opposite direction. For example, in Erika's urban Hispanic gang subculture, teen pregnancy, violence, and gang wars were a part of the lived experiences of middle school students. In this culture, at their age, these topics were significant and therefore culturally relevant and age-appropriate pedagogy that would allow for learning that addresses such issues.

This approach to choosing texts would help with the well-documented achievement gap, which is discussed further in Chapter 9. Marginalized students in particular need texts that reflect their life experiences. When we, as teachers, choose texts for our classrooms, we must stop and analyze whose voices we are privileging and whose voices are left out or marginalized. "Advocating for higher literacy achievement for all students, although a worthwhile goal in its own right, has the potential for even greater impact when adolescents' identity-making practices are taken into consideration and their voices are invited to the table for discussion" (Alvermann et al, 2006, p. xxiii). Such practices would help all students to find spaces in the classroom and ownership of the learning process. It would help all voices, including those outside of the hegemonic culture, to be valued and heard. bell hooks (1994) noted, "To begin, the [teacher]) must genuinely value everyone's presence. There must be an ongoing recognition that everyone influences the classroom dynamic, that everyone contributes. These contributions are resources. Used constructively, they enhance the capacity of any class to create an open learning environment" (p. 8). Valuing everyone's presence begins with valuing everyone's life experiences.

The middle school curriculum needs to include real conversations about topics of concern to adolescents in general and, more importantly, to the specific students in each classroom. The curriculum should emerge from the needs and interests of the students. Skill development should be built upon that base rather than focusing on a pre-set list of facts or standards or test questions to the exclusion of everything else.

When children begin school — in preschool, kindergarten, or early childhood care — teachers and caregivers are more willing to include the whole child and their out-of-school experiences in school conversations. Though issues of violence or prison or sexuality are seen as taboo at every level, it is not unusual to enter a preschool or kindergarten classroom and observe the students reading books about their cultural holidays, talking about their families or their pets, drawing pictures of what they ate for breakfast, or discussing a trip to the grocery store or their new shoes.

However, by the time students reach middle school, such conversations about their real lives are relegated to passing periods, lunchtime, notes passed during class, and out-of-school texts like teen magazines, e-mails, or blogs. But the underlying pedagogical strategies used in early childhood should also translate into the later years of learning.

In Sprague and Keeling's (2007) *Discovering Their Voices: Engaging Adolescent Girls with Young Adult Literature,* the authors call the genre that deals with issues such as teen violence, sexuality, and other real-life teen experiences "contemporary realistic young adult fiction." In this genre, the reader follows characters as they wrestle with real issues, like violence or abuse. This genre allows readers to think about deeper universal themes like struggle, conflict, and love, promoting problem solving and higher-order thinking. Using texts that include violence as a theme can "serve as a lens to help us see how violence functions in our collective imagination" (Franzak & Noll, 2006, p. 671). Explorations of the causes and preventions of violence of any kind would help students read violence as a complex text that must be wrestled with on the path to building a quality adult life.

Although these young adult fiction texts are available, it doesn't mean that they are making their way into classrooms or school libraries.

In *Struggling Adolescent Readers* (Moore, Alvermann, & Hinchman, 2000), one researcher found that most school and classroom libraries have a limited number of student-preferred materials and many teachers must use their own money to purchase materials that are "not obviously relevant to the school's curriculum" (p. 234). Similarly, Ms. Carpenter had to order or buy many of her independent reading books herself because the school librarian wouldn't buy them. She explained, "I just want them to be reading as much as possible. . . . I order a lot of books from Scholastic as class books because [the librarian] won't order them. . . . I try really hard to give kids books that I think they'll relate to on some level."

Administrators, librarians, support staff, and parents need to support teachers in promoting pedagogical practices that will lead to improved learning for all students. We need those involved in the education of our children at every level—principals, parents, librarians, teachers, counselors—to support a pedagogy that allows children to read texts that are developmentally appropriate. We all need to support our students by providing them with compelling texts that resonate with their lives. We need to take risks to confront a status quo that does not serve our students and, instead, reach toward methods that will create positive change, develop learners, and promote authentic growth.

CHAPTER 7

Technology and Creativity: How Multiple Literacies Can Build Educational Resiliency

Multiple literacies is a framework for thinking about literacy. Multiple literacies expands the notion of literacy from a one-dimensional concept to one that is marked by multiplicity, diversity, and complexity. It is a repudiation of earlier notions of literacy that focused exclusively on reading and writing with school as a primary site and instead an acknowledgment that literacy has many forms, sites, and types of texts and practices.

This chapter focuses on three ways that the girls used multiple literacies to build educational resiliency. Resiliency can be defined as "an individual successfully adapting to stressful circumstances and conditions" (Evans-Winters, 2005, p. 110). Educational resiliency refers to the likelihood of success in school despite adversities. Tetra and Kaliya used technology to build connections to marginalized identities, and such connections are seen as factors that promote resiliency in the lives of students. Moniqua, Erika, and Tetra used creative writing and drawing to develop their voices, also a contributing attribute to building educational resiliency. All of these literacy sites were outside of the regular classroom. All are examples of girls using multiple literacies to adapt to stressful circumstances and build personal agency.

USING THE INTERNET AS A LITERACY PRACTICE THAT BUILDS RESILIENCY

The Internet was a primary text for all of the students in the Girls Literacy Discussion Group. However, there was a range of access available and time devoted to Internet use. Girls of this age have been called a part of the millennial generation, which is considered to be the first generation of digital natives. However, it is incorrect to paint all youth of this generation as tech-savvy, fluent in multiple digital literacies and constantly connected to their iPhones, iPads, iPods, or other up-and-coming technologies. Farmer (2008) pointed out:

> With all the talk about the millennial generation and its tech-saaviness, it is all too easy for adults to assume that these young people need little instruction or encouragement in using technology. The reality is much more nuanced. The telephone is still the technology of choice for teens. Nine-tenths of teens are wired, but almost half seldom use the Internet. While the majority of telecommunicators are now female, they remain underrepresented in technology careers. Indeed, not every teenager embraces technology, sometimes because of poverty. (p. 1)

Of the girls in the Girls Literacy Discussion Group, four of the six had Internet access in their homes. Regarding their Internet usage, they described searching for information, using e-mail and instant messaging, writing fan fiction, watching music videos, downloading photos and music, and playing online video games. Because this research was conducted in 2004 and digital media and trends shift quickly, I contacted the language arts teacher at Lincoln Middle School to see what has changed. She reported that the biggest shift has been the use of Facebook, which she said is used by about 50% of both male and female students at Lincoln Middle School. She also said that access to technology is still a significant issue, with about 25% of students having no computer or Internet access at home or anywhere else outside of school.

For the girls in this book, the overwhelming majority of the time spent on the Internet was outside of school. Other research has also documented this finding. "Tech-savvy teens report that their most fruitful uses of the Internet take place outside school walls" (Black & Steinkuehler, 2009, p. 272). In fact, I never saw any of the girls use a computer at school except for one who took a computer class. In this way, digital literacies were literacy practices unmeasured and unacknowledged by school assessments.

The girls were not isolated in their interactions with technology. Previous studies have viewed technology as belonging exclusively to youth and baffling adults. As Dimitriadis (2001) wrote: "Young people today are using ever ubiquitous media forms and technologies to define and map their daily lives in ways that often confound adults, including teachers" (p. 2). On the contrary, these girls used both technologies and media forms *with* their parents rather than separate from them. Tetra, Kaliya, and Angela's parents helped their daughters learn how to use both e-mail and the Internet. Kaliya explained, "[My mom's] a computer person. She builds computers. She's like really into computers. That's how I got my e-mail.

My mom got it for me." Likewise, Tetra noted, "My mom, my dad, and my sister, we all use the computer and we all use Internet. My mom and dad live on e-mail."

A primary role of the Internet was as a source for information. For example, Erika used the computers at her grandmother's house and at school to download pictures of her favorite hip-hop musicians, Angela liked to look at her daily horoscope on the web, and Moniqua used the Internet to find out which movies were showing at the mall. Tetra used computers for reading and writing fan fiction, and Kaliya liked to watch video clips of her favorite musicians.

In addition, Tetra and Kaliya both used the Internet to strengthen their connections to marginalized and minority communities. "The Internet is uniquely suited to the predicaments of youth who are often geographically separated, culturally isolated and socially threatened" (Driver, 2007, p. 170). Tetra was a young lesbian/bisexual in a school with no other out students, and Kaliya was an African American girl in a school with few Black students, so they both faced issues of marginalization and alienation. The Internet served as a conduit to larger communities, counteracting the physical isolation.

Tetra came out as a lesbian in the 7th grade and had faced homophobic harassment at school ever since. "There are lots of homophobic people here," she told me. I asked for an example and she replied, "Every time I get in line [in the cafeteria], if there's someone who doesn't want to stand next to me because I'm bisexual, they'll be like, 'I don't want to stand by the fag!'" But Tetra didn't remain silent. "I'm like, 'Shut up! Go away! If you don't want to stand by me, get out of line! I want my food!'"

Tetra had spoken up several times about the homophobia at school. "At the beginning of the year I didn't say anything, and then through part of the year I started noticing that every 3 seconds I'd hear someone say 'fag' or 'faggot.' I didn't know if they were directing it at me or not, but it was really starting to offend me." Tetra took the issue to her class meeting. "I got up and announced to the class that I don't like it when people use the word 'gay' as a synonym for 'stupid,' and I don't like it when people say 'fag' or 'faggot' or 'lezzie' or 'dyke' when they're putting it in a mean context." Unfortunately, Tetra's experience was not unique. GLSEN's *2009 School Climate Study* found that 61.1% of LGBT students felt unsafe at their school because of their sexual orientation, 84.6% were verbally harassed, and 52.9% were harassed via electronic mediums (cyberbullying). Thirty percent had skipped a day of school in the past month due to feeling unsafe at school (Kosciw, Greytak, Diaz, & Bartkiewicz, 2010).

I asked Tetra whether her speaking out made a difference. "Since then nobody really uses those words except a certain group of boys who always joke about gay people and how it's sick and wrong," she explained. "It's very annoying because I always somehow manage to be sitting two desks away from them. So I'm always looking over and glaring at them."

In the Girls Literacy Discussion Group, Tetra didn't discuss her sexual identification except for a couple of subtle hints here and there. At one point, she referred to herself as an "oddball"; said that her favorite show was *Will & Grace*—the only prime-time sitcom at the time with gay characters—and said that her favorite movie was *Hedwig and the Angry Inch,* an independent film about a male-to-female transsexual.

In an individual interview, I asked Tetra why she didn't bring up being lesbian or bisexual in the group. She replied, "I was trying not to because I know that all the other girls have been like, 'There she goes again, talking about this!' They're probably so annoyed with me." I asked her if she didn't want me to bring it up in the group. "Oh no!" she exclaimed, "I am so open about that. I talk about that all the time. Just so you know." However, in our group, she never did end up talking openly about being lesbian.

Tetra had tried to meet other lesbians her age. In 7th grade, she and her friend Timothy started a Gay Straight Alliance at the school. "Timothy was like, 'They have all sorts of clubs here. We should just start a club!' So we were thinking about it and mentioned it and somehow Ms. Giroux heard about it and so she and Ms. Carpenter started it, and now we have a GSA." The group had up to 15 members in attendance at a time, but Tetra was the only openly gay student. "I'm the only openly gay person in the GSA 'cause you don't have to say if you are or you aren't."

Even today, lesbian, gay, bisexual, and transgender youth commonly face social isolation and loneliness as they struggle to find support and community (Kosciw et al., 2010; Payne & Smith, 2011; Wilkinson & Pearson, 2009). Tetra described some of her difficulty making friends:

> I was a tomboy, and I preferred to play football over playing with dolls, and I had GI Joe. . . . I've never had that many friends who were girls just because I think that I do tend to scare them away a little bit. Even if they don't think that I'm a lesbian or anything, it's just too weird for them that there's a girl who just doesn't care at all about what she looks like. I have scared away tons of people that way, so most of my friends are male.

Then, as far as her male friends go, she said, "The one bad thing about having friends that are guys, [is that in] my entire life, people, if they don't assume that I'm a lesbian, they assume that I'm going out with my male friends." She said that her friend Matthew "had a very hard time being my friend and Roberto got teased a lot for being my friend, and Jake got teased for being my friend. . . . So, that's the one bad thing about having a lot of male friends." Tetra continued, "I kind of feel bad for them. . . . It really did hurt Matthew's feelings, but he didn't stop being my friend. He didn't stop playing with me or anything." These struggles took a toll on Tetra (see Figure 7.1).

For Tetra, the Internet was her primary tool for finding support on her coming-out journey. She used the Internet to do "research" on what it meant to be a lesbian. Tetra explained, "My research consisted of typing up [on the Internet], like trying to find gay and lesbian youth organizations. I noticed that a lot of the places I went to would be like 'gay lesbian bisexual transgender' or something like that." When terms came up that she didn't understand, she used the Internet to find out more information. She explained "I would look and I started noticing that bisexuality was up there a ton and I didn't know what it was. So one day I just went to the dictionary on the Internet and it said 'bisexuality' and came up with the [definition]." Here Tetra demonstrated a critical literacy perspective as she critiqued the online dictionary:

Figure 7.1. Tetra's Writing

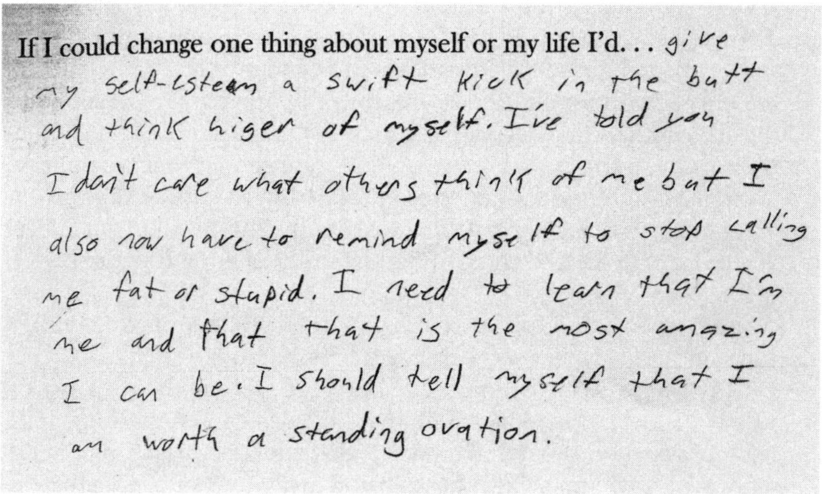
If I could change one thing about myself or my life I'd. . . give my self-esteem a swift kick in the butt and think higer of myself. I've told you I don't care what others think of me but I also now have to remind myself to stop calling me fat or stupid. I need to learn that I'm me and that that is the most amazing I can be. I should tell myself that I am worth a standing ovation.

If I could change one thing about myself or my life I'd . . . give my self-esteem a swift kick in the butt and think higher of myself. I've told you I don't care what others think about me, but I also have to remind myself to stop calling me fat or stupid. I need to learn that I'm me and that is the most amazing I can be. I should tell myself that I am worth a standing ovation.

> I think the thing that pisses me off the most about the dictionary and their descriptions is that "heterosexuals" are a male and female who love each other and "homosexuality" are two people who are dating or seeing each other. It never mentions love. In the dictionary, it does not mention love. And so that pisses me off.

Tetra's mother used the Internet to order books with lesbian themes from Amazon.com for Tetra. After she came out to her mother, "My mom ordered about ten books about the experiences of being lesbian" Tetra explained. "She bought me *Deliver Us from Evie* and *Annie on My Mind* . . . so now we have a tiny little stack of gay and lesbian books in the dining room."

Tetra said that she was first exposed to lesbians on Internet fan fiction sites. "I was already reading slash and yayo male-male and female-female stories; slash is when there are two guys going out or two females going out and yayo is the same thing but it's more of an art and NC-17 [rated as no one under 17 may view] thing," Tetra explained to me. Fan fiction opened her mind to positive images of lesbians. "Through fan fiction I learned a little more about that so my picture of a lesbian was any woman. It was just like anyone." These Internet texts provided Tetra windows into a queer world. "The websites I go to that have to deal with gay and lesbian issues are mainly fandom sites like Strawberry Swirl. It's a whole Harry Potter lesbian site." She added that now she writes her own lesbian fan fiction, which she posts on Internet fan fiction sites.

Fan fiction is an example of the new literacies that permeate adolescent lives (Black & Steinkuehler, 2009; Warburten, 2010). As of this writing, Harry Potter was the most popular book topic on www.fanfiction.net, with over 500,000 stories. Black and Steinkuehler (2009) commented on fan fiction:

> The ubiquity and sheer number of fan-fiction texts make it a difficult phenomenon to overlook. Moreover the fact that much of this fiction is being written and read by adolescents makes it a fascinating topic for education and literacy researchers who seek to understand the role of new media and on line communication technologies in youth's literate, social and academic worlds. (p. 274)

For Tetra, fan fiction illuminated a queer world that she didn't have access to in her "real" life. She could even be part of that world, not only as an observer but as a participant by writing and posting her own lesbian Harry Potter fan fiction.

The Internet played a significant role for Tetra in developing an emergent sense of community. While fan fiction first exposed her to the idea of lesbians, the Internet allowed her access to conversations with lesbians. As social networking grows, the Internet is more and more playing a unique role in the development of adolescents' social spheres. "Because Internet communication, in particular, is overtly social in nature, it offers an environment in which young people create identities that allow them to enter the textual worlds they want to join" (Lewis & Del Valle, 2009, p. 314). Although Tetra didn't have any lesbian friends in her "real" life, she said that "over the Internet I have met a few lesbians."

"When you talk to people, do they know that you are 14?" I asked.

"Um," Tetra replied. "A lot of them don't." She quickly added, "But if they say 'How old are you?' I'll say I'm a 14-year-old." She paused. "I think that usually shocks a lot of them," she added.

Tetra then told me how both she and her straight sister "enjoy" talking with older men and women on the Internet who may not realize that they are only 14- and 16-year-old girls:

But my sister who's 16 . . . she'll talk to someone (on the web) and he'll think she's 28 or something. . . . She had a guy once who was trying to talk to her and she was trying to ignore him because he wanted to hook up with her over the Internet and he probably lives in Mississippi or something. When he asked her, "Oh baby, how old are you?" she was like "How old are you?" He was like, "I'm 32," and she was like, "Oh, that's too bad. I'm 15." The guy stopped talking to her after that.

Tetra laughed before saying, "It's very funny. We enjoy doing that when we know that someone thinks that we're older than we really are."

Although these Internet encounters could be seen as risky or dangerous behaviors, I did not see these actions as placing Tetra in a dangerous situation. Tetra was a girl who was relatively sheltered from the outer adult and even teen world. She did not go to the under-21 dances or clubs as did several of the other girls. She did not even go to the local under-21 LBGT group, although she expressed interest in finding out more about it. The only social event she ever mentioned attending was a high school basketball game with her older sister. The Internet, like romance novels or other fictional sources, allowed Tetra and her sister to dabble in the "exotic" adult world of seduction and rendezvous without actually leaving the safety of their comfortable middle-class living room.

Tetra and her sister's choice to meet people on the Internet and misrepresent themselves was an indication that the girls wished to be powerful independent meaning-makers and agents of their own sexuality, and, on their own, they were, though perhaps clumsily, attempting to do so. In the face of limitations, silences, stereotypes, and labels, these girls were trying to find spaces where they could assert themselves as sexual subjects by creating their own (albeit problematic) texts. For Tetra, who faced homophobic verbal harassment and isolation as both a lesbian and a butch girl, the Internet helped her build a sense of belonging she did not have in her school world.

Similarly, Kaliya used the Internet as a way to build connections to an African American community that was nearly nonexistent in her school. Lincoln Middle School, which was mostly Hispanic and White students, had a small population of Black students, less than 5%. In individual interviews, Kaliya indicated some of the difficulties of being African American at a school with such a small Black population. She explained, "I kind of like it better in Houston. They're not racists here, but sometimes you feel left out because there's a lot of people here who's not your culture." Kaliya's favorite TV show was *College Hill*, a reality show set at an all-Black university. Kaliya remarked, "I like it because it's kind of cool. . . . When I get older, I want to go to an all-Black college."

In the Girls Literacy Discussion Group, Kaliya had never mentioned any interest in computers or technology, but on the day I took the girls to the computer lab, I witnessed Kaliya's ease with computer technology. All of the pictures Kaliya downloaded were images of African Americans, from photographs e-mailed from her cousins to hip-hop musicians. I was struck by the visually significant contrast between the racial world she saw around her at school and the one she could access on the Internet. Mahiri (2001) commented on the "multicultural" nature of the Internet, where pop culture producers of color "e-merge on the information highway" without suffering "the same targeted, racist indignities during electronic travel as they currently do in 'driving while black'" (p. 383). For Kaliya, as an African American girl, the Internet could transcend geography, bringing her to Black communities while she was still physically situated in a predominantly White and Hispanic environment.

One of Kaliya's favorite Internet activities was accessing music. Music acted as a text that supported her developing identities. For all the girls, music, like fashion, was used as an identity marker. Most of the girls listed their favorite music when they were describing themselves, and several of them mentioned having posters of singers, such as Nelly, Chingy, and B2K, in their bedrooms. Kaliya said that in her room she had a "rest in peace area" for Aaliyah and Lisa "Left Eye" Lopes. "The musical style selected was not simply an expression of what they liked but who they were. Not simply who they were but also who they would be. It was a dialectic exploration of 'being' and 'becoming' at the same moment, identity as process" (Bloustein, 2003, p. 231). In this way, access to music was crucial in supporting Kaliya's sense of self as a girl of color.

Music did not just mark a personal identity but also indicated belonging to certain school social groups. Although their engagement with music was an out-of-school literacy, students still referred to musical preferences, performers, and clubs during the school day. While the school had music classes such as band, chorus, and orchestra, with the exception of one participant, Tetra, when the girls were discussing music as a text, they were referring exclusively to music they listened to outside of school. Music devices such as MP3 players were not allowed in school during the school day. For example, Kaliya indicated that membership in her school social group revolved around a particular under-21 dance scene: "Most of us like going to dances, not school dances, like the M Mix or Sand Dune or something." Again, these musical and social group alliances were interfused with race and class identifications as well. "Youth [music] affiliations are very much micro-cultural, simply aged, gendered and ethnically nuanced perspectives and distillations of their larger parent cultures" (Bloustein, 2003, p. 222). For example, the girls of color listed hip-hop and R&B as their favorite kinds of music. Tetra, the only White girl in the Girls Literacy Discussion Group, did not indicate an interest in these musical styles but instead preferred classical music. Therefore, taste in music was used to indicate belonging to a group as well as a particular construction of self. For Kaliya, access to music links, music videos, and music downloads, like her other Internet activity, served to support her identity as a girl of color and give her access to an African American community and culture that was hardly accessible at Lincoln Middle School.

For both of these students, the Internet provided a connection to distant and online communities that helped mitigate some of the isolation each of these marginalized girls experienced, thereby enhancing their personal resiliency. Of the girls in the Girls Literacy Discussion Group, both Kaliya and Tetra were academically motivated students with above-average test scores and grade point averages. Both girls were solidly middle class, which put them on a higher economic level than many of the other students at the school. Both girls had parents who were professionals and, perhaps more importantly, mothers who were professionals and computer-savvy and supportive of their daughters in their engagement with the Internet. Both girls had computers and Internet access at home.

Both girls also had significant social networks at school. The social cliques at the school were primarily split by race and personal interests. Tetra's social circle was what she called "the band geeks," an almost exclusively White group of students who played instruments in either the school band or school orchestra. Kaliya's group was all students of color, mostly "Spanish" as noted by another girl in the group, who enjoyed listening to pop music and going to the local under-21 club and the mall. Their Internet connections did not replace social interaction with peers but instead seemed to fill in the gaps that they were unable to fill at the school.

USING MULTIPLE LITERACIES TO CREATE
THEIR OWN TEXTS

A crucial step for girls in making meaning of themselves in their worlds is having a space to find their voices. Girls are surrounded by texts that convey messages about gender and sexuality—from the mass media, from school, from church, from friends, and from parents. As meaning-makers, they interact with these texts and construct identity performances based on their understandings of these textual experiences. As they read their worlds, they also need spaces to tell their stories, share their own narratives, and create their own texts. As bell hooks (1989) wrote, "Moving from silence into speech is . . . a gesture of defiance that heals, that makes new life and new growth possible. It is that act of speech, of 'talking back' that is no mere gesture of empty words, that is the expression of our movement from object to subject—the liberated voice" (p. 9). These girls were at the beginning of that process, of finding their voices as young women.

When discussing what they liked to write on their own, the girls mentioned that they created texts that addressed issues of sexuality, love, and bodies. Their writing indicates that these areas are of importance to girls as they use the texts around them to help them construct their own definitions of self, including a sense of sexual self. These texts were emergent and sometimes tentative. Nevertheless, the girls demonstrated beginning literacies of sexual empowerment, ones that will serve them as they continue to grow and develop and make meaning of themselves as sexual beings in the world.

Early in the semester, I asked the girls what they liked to write. Although she rarely handed in any written schoolwork, Erika revealed that she and her boyfriend exchanged letters, e-mails, and poetry. "I try to write poems. Like I made one; it was about a boy and a girl," Erika told me, looking down at the desk.

Erika was not willing to share the poetry, possibly an indication of the poetry being a space of intimacy between Erika and her boyfriend. "He writes me love poems," she explained. "It's cute."

Tetra told me that she wrote her own lesbian fan fiction. Like Erika, she was not willing to share the actual writing with me, but she did encourage me to visit www.fanfiction.net, the site where she posted her writing and read writing similar to her own.

Moniqua was the one student willing to share her poetry with me, including poems to her boyfriend. Moniqua used her literacies to create texts that, while not explicitly sexual, addressed her feelings and struggles with intimate relationships, the meaning of love, and issues like divorce and breaking up. For example, one of Moniqua's poems started: "I wonder why." It continued:

> I wonder why marriages seem to fail
> Is it because husbands cheat
> Is it because they have arguments
> Or because of their ugly feet?

Although the poem has lightness and humor, it also raises the difficult issue of divorce, a significant theme for this group of girls. Of the six girls in the Girls Literacy Discussion Group, only two lived with both of their parents. Moniqua, who used her poem to investigate the issue of divorce, had not seen her father since she was 3 years old.

Moniqua said that she enjoyed writing, especially poetry. She gave me a stack of poems and pictures she had created over the last couple of years. "I have a whole book full [of poems]," she told me in our first individual interview. Most of the poems she showed me were accompanied by black-and-white pencil drawings. These artifacts, as well as the drawings I saw her do in class, indicated that Moniqua both enjoyed her creative and artistic literacies and was quite talented in this area. She told me that she planned to take Art 1 in high school because she "likes drawing."

Moniqua didn't keep her poems to herself but shared them with her peers. "Kaliya's read them, Erika's read them, a whole bunch of people have read them . . . do you want me to bring them next time?" she offered. Moniqua and her boyfriend had broken up during the course of the semester, and her poems reflected some of her feelings around the relationship. Here is one of her poems (Figure 7.2).

A central theme in Moniqua's poetry was love and the emotions surrounding it. By creating her own texts about her experiences, Moniqua created a space for her own voice about such topics, ones that are most often not integrated into the school-sanctioned curriculum. Although schools often claim to focus on literacy, they often neglect to include creative forms such as art, poetry, dance, music, and movement in their formal literacy curriculum. However, we see here that such creative expressions were a central part of Moniqua's literacy practices. An understanding of the multiplicity of literacy practices allows us to see how creative forms are an integral part of students' literacies. "The full range of adolescent literacy is much more complex, dynamic and sophisticated than what is traditionally encompassed within school-sanctioned literate activity" (Alvermann et al., 1998, p. 1). Moniqua's poetry exemplified one of her multiple literacies, that of creative expression. Moniqua's poetry about her emotions reflected a vulnerability I didn't often see with her.

Figure 7.2. Vanished Poem

Vanished

I've vanished now
From your dark mind.
I don't exist,
Been left behind.
Just memory.
No gentle grade.
No perfect curves.
Of your sweet face.
I know I've vanished.
It's sad but true.
But I still seem to keep.
The memory of you.

Black Tears

Little black tears streamed down her face
And little black diamonds took their place
She wiped her eyes
Her face was flushed
And little by little
Her cries were hushed.

Moniqua's writing gave evidence of her own process of meaning-making of herself and the world around her. As seen in Moniqua's poem in the Introduction (p. 1), her writing had some of the complexities and contradictions of her own identity performances, including her body as a text. This poem demonstrates her awareness of some of the "hybridities and ambiguities" that characterize the postmodern era of identity construction (Anzaldúa & Keating, 2002, p. 3). She recognized a dissonance between her inside self and the one that she presented to the outer world. In her poetry and her drawings, Moniqua created texts that reflected this inner world. By sharing the texts with her friends, teachers, and me, she was building bridges between these inner and outer worlds and identities.

Moniqua's critical and intellectual intensity was matched by her creative expressions of art and poetry. Monique used her expressive literacies to help her in the process of meaning-making of herself and the world around her. Her poetry and art centered on her experiences in the world. As a creator of text, Moniqua took the power of creation and representation and held it in her own hands. By writing poetry, posting fan fiction, and creating their own stories, these girls were beginning to find their voices and working to create their own narratives. These steps reflected significant elements of educational resiliency, including self-determination and a sense of personal agency.

IMPLICATIONS AND RECOMMENDATIONS

Current media headlines focusing on girls and the Internet highlight the dangers of mixing adolescent girls and technology. Horror stories of cyberbullying, sexting, and sexual predators on the Web dominate mainstream representations of girls and the Internet. Research on middle school girls and technology tends to focus on the digital divide—how girls' use of technology compares to boys' or how low-income students' access to technology compares to that of higher-income students. While there is a consensus that middle school classrooms and curricula should include technology, there is still a great need for further understanding of how to integrate technology in a way that supports middle school students' growth.

The students in the Girls Literacy Discussion Group used the Internet as a tool to gain information, build resiliency, develop ties to community, and enrich their lives. The Internet, as a text, had a positive role in their multiple literacies. Their relationship with technology was not one of passive consumer but of co-creator. This experience of young people using technology in personal, dynamic, and ever-shifting ways is becoming more and more prevalent.

As teachers, we cannot ignore these significant texts that play an enormous role in the lives of our students. Like the mass media, the technological texts with which students engage form a hidden curriculum that runs as an undercurrent throughout their days. As parents and teachers, we must not allow alarmist media messages to cause us to be frightened of the Internet but instead view it as a text with which our students have a transactional relationship. As discussed in this chapter, because the media and Internet are so pervasive in the lives of children today, the middle school curriculum must include extensive lessons on critical media literacy development, including extensive focus on the Internet, texting, social media, and other hypermedia forms.

This chapter speaks to the need for a feminist critical literacy curriculum focusing on technology in middle school classrooms. As girls like Tetra and Kaliya navigate the Internet, they need space to deconstruct the images and information they find there, they need the skills to safely navigate spaces, and they need the opportunity to have critical conversations like the one that Tetra began about the bias found in the online dictionary.

They need to be taught how to deconstruct and challenge any text that comes their way, including e-mail, tweets, and Facebook posts. Issues of self-representation, audience, and voice are paramount. As girls seek to explore the meaning of gender, race, femininity, sexual orientation, and gender expression, they need educators and mentors who can help them learn how to develop a critical perspective toward their engagement with digital texts and literacy engagements.

Such learning begins with bringing these texts into the classroom. In these "new times" when middle school students' everyday lives are intertwined with technology, as educators we must view literacy in its multiplicity and examine how our students use their diverse literacy experiences such as the Internet in sophisticated and complicated ways. In this case, students used the Internet to further their sense of agency and build community. In particular, for marginalized students who are disengaged learners, the Internet was a tool for building community, combating isolation, and supporting personal growth. These strengths provided by digital literacies can be harnessed by educators as we seek to build connections between out-of-school texts and the in-school curriculum. For example, classroom discussions can be forums where students talk about what sites they like to visit, how they use Facebook in their lives, or how to share fan fiction. In breaking down walls between in-school and out-of-school literacy experiences, as educators we will have greater opportunities to engage students, especially marginalized learners. In 1983, Richard Byrne, director of the Center for Media Literacy, wrote: "The technology is not the revolution. The revolution is in human awareness and aliveness. It is just made clearer by technology." We can help our students develop a critical consciousness as they use technological tools on their journey of awareness and aliveness.

As the girls in the Girls Literacy Discussion Group found and created their own texts, they used these literacy practices to further develop the construction of their sense of self. These self-made texts stood alongside the cacophony of texts that permeated their lives. Feminist theorists call for the creation of women-made media and texts as a response to the negative images in mainstream media and texts. Rebecca Walker (2003) called for "new scripts . . . based not on what the culture dictates but on what we have come to know and experience in the intimate moments of our day to day lives" (p. xvii). Likewise, Carla Stokes (2010) in her research on Black girls and the Internet, called for "culturally specific safe spaces for girls to construct their own media that challenges sexualization and hegemonic gender roles and promotes self-worth that encompasses the whole person" (p. 64). These acts of self-creation are acts of resistance and empowerment for young women.

In my middle school language arts classroom, I include media-making as part of the curriculum. Students are given options such as making their own video, making their own commercial, or creating their own print advertisement. Sometimes when there is a conflict in the classroom or school community, I have had students conduct video interviews with other students representing divergent viewpoints. Together, the students then watch these media creations made by themselves and one another. I have found that even the most disengaged student comes alive when you give him or her a video camera or a place in front of the camera to explore a topic he or she feels passionate about.

Especially with new forms of media, more and more students are engaged in not only media consumption but also media production. Whether it's creating blogs, posting videos on YouTube, sharing notes on Facebook, using electronic bulletin boards or other forms of Internet information sharing, youth today have so many more options for media production as well as access to diverse audiences. "In this new media age . . . children move among modes and media, making and transforming meanings and demonstrating tremendous flexibility and creativity in their use of cultural tools" (Stornaiuolo, Hull, & Nelson, 2009, p. 384). Again, understanding multiple literacies as a particularly useful framework for middle school learners, we can see that text production is a form of literacy. These creative texts can be both a form of self-expressions and a form of assessment when they are valued by the teacher as a form of multiple literacy practices. Teachers can create bridges between media production outside the classroom and in school literacy activities and assessments.

CHAPTER 8

Multiple Literacies and a Failing Student

Erika was a failing student. She scored low on her standardized tests. Her standardized reading test scores placed her in the 25th percentile, just above the cutoff to be held back. She was failing several subject areas, including language arts. Erika rarely turned in any of her assignments. Because she handed in so little work, her language arts teacher found it hard to assess her abilities. During silent reading time in class, Erika would read to herself, but the teacher was "unsure" if she understood what she was reading.

In class, Erika sat silently with her head on her desk, her long hair strewn across her face, until a teacher came by and told her to sit up. Michelle Fine has called this posture "the physical embodiment of silencing in urban schools" (Fine & Weis, 2003, p. 34). Erika rarely spoke during class. She was a silent and disengaged learner.

I came to find that beyond her test scores and failing grades, Erika demonstrated significant literacy practices that had slipped under the radar of traditional assessment. She used the Internet to find information and communicate with others; she had extensive knowledge of the oral history of her family; she was involved with her church community, including reading religious texts; and she enjoyed reading and writing at home. In these ways, Erika demonstrated to me several forms of literacies that were not part of her literacy assessments at school.

ERIKA'S LITERACY PRACTICES

Erika demonstrated significant literacy skills and abilities that slipped under the radar of traditional assessment. Using a model of multiple literacies, we can see the complexities of Erika's experience with multiple texts and ways of knowing. "This research [on multiple literacies] has begun to help us recognize that school-sponsored literacy is but one way of being literate in our society and around the world" (Huot, Stroble, &

Bazerman, 2004, p. 4). In this framework, literacies take multiple forms in multiple sites. Erika was a girl who enjoyed engaging in literacy activities. She told me that she enjoyed reading and writing. She liked to read "e-mails, magazines, and books," including reading *Teen Magazine,* about which she said, "My mom buys them, so I read them when she gets them." She said she liked to read "in my room" where "it's quiet." The books she liked to read included *Roll of Thunder, Hear My Cry,* and *Glory Field,* both of which she read for language arts class. Erika also told me, "I like writing." She explained further, "When I'm bored and I don't have nothing to do and I don't feel like reading, then I'll just write my friend a note or just write something on a piece of paper." She said, "I feel like I'm good at it [writing]. But not really, because sometimes when I'm mad or something, I misspell words. And I get really mad and I scratch it out and then I start writing it again." She said that she always liked writing "From first writing my ABCs. From then on I was writing letters, letters after letters [to friends] . . . but I get caught sometimes." She had written poetry. When I asked if it was an assignment, she replied, "I just did it on my own." She bashfully revealed that she read it to her boyfriend. "He thought it was good and I was like, 'No, it's not! Shut up!'"

Erika also used technology both to gain information and to e-mail her boyfriend. She did not have a computer at her house but said, "I usually go to my auntie's house because she lives right next to me. On Sundays and Saturdays I go to my nana's and I play the computer there. I like to go to websites and e-mail." On the day our group worked in the computer lab, I was able to observe Erika's digital literacies. She quickly turned on the computer, got online, and then headed straight for the websites of her favorite singers, Ashanti and Chingy. "I like going on BET and all them," she said proudly. "Like, if you go to www.chingy.com, they have Chingy and it shows a bunch of pictures of him!" Sure enough, she spent the hour in the computer lab downloading and printing pictures of her favorite musicians.

Music was significant to Erika. She enjoyed singing and was in the school chorus, which was one of the elective classes 8th-grade students could select. She said that chorus class was "fun" and she liked learning different songs. When she was at home, she liked to sing. "When I'm by myself, I sing to myself. When I'm on the phone with my boyfriend and I start singing, [my family] is like 'Shut up!'" she said with a laugh.

When examining the literacy practices of students, we must look not only at the school-based literacies but also at those rooted in the home and community. "In reality, the school is but one site of learning children encounter in their lives. The cultures of home, church and community have a tremendous impact on the identity development of children and the literacy practices encountered in these sites" (Kelly, 2001, p. 243). For Erika, this issue was particularly salient. Erika was rooted in the rural Hispanic community where her family had lived for generations. There she took part in local festivals, church events, and family gatherings. Erika could speak and understand Spanish, though English was her first and primary language. Erika said that she liked to go to church, which she attended every Sunday with her grandmother and aunt. She attended religious school and studied for her First Communion. There she read the Bible and studied prayers, explaining, "Like if some people don't know the Ten Commandments or the seven sacraments, then they gotta teach them about it and stuff and that's what we do." She was looking forward to picking her *madrina* (godmother) for her confirmation and going to classes again, where "you go there and stay there like an hour 'til 7:00 and then you study what you're going to be doing." These literacy practices were not seen by the school but were central in her life.

Despite her complex, sophisticated, and compelling multiple literacies, Erika was positioned in the school as lacking sufficient literacy and at risk of being a future drop-out. Her teacher labeled her as a "struggling reader." This term, a more recent adaptation of terms such as *slow* or *at risk*, indicates "youth with clinically diagnosed reading disabilities as well as those who are unmotivated, in remediation, disenchanted, or generally unsuccessful in school literacy tasks" (Alvermann, 2001, p. 680). The terms result in a positioning or labeling of students. "Terms like at risk or remedial permit the institution of the school to position these students as failures, and as persons likely to continue to fail, unlikely to fit into the system, and inevitably, persons who will suffer sanctions for nonconformity" (O'Brian, Springs, & Stith, 2001, p. 106). In this sense, Erika was framed for failure.

Studies have documented how being labeled a failure, behind, or a slow reader affects how readers see themselves as literate beings. Alvermann (2001) noted that "readers locked into 'special' identifications know all too well which side of the enabling or disabling binary they occupy and the consequences such identities carry" (p. 678). Erika had already been positioned as a special education student, retained in 4th grade as failing to perform, and now, in 8th grade, as a struggling reader with low test performance. "The ways that people experience the world and are positioned in it shape both their access to literacy and how they engage in various literacies and other discursive practices" (O'Brian, Moje, & Stewart, 2001, p. 45). These positionings, in turn, shaped how she positioned herself in terms of literacy, particularly in terms of her in-school literacy identity.

Research has indicated that students who are labeled slow or failures may disengage from classroom literacy learning (Easton, 2008). O'Brian and colleagues (2001) remarked, "Early in their academic histories, students who are currently labeled as at risk experienced failure and developed early dispositions towards school that helped them avoid failure and preserve their self esteem" (p. 109). One way this position emerges is the avoidance of tasks at which students perceive they will fail. As Alvermann (2001) described:

> When these youth find the school's institutionalized practices of reading and writing irrelevant and at odds with their motivation to learn, they typically look for ways to avoid such practices. Often, their avoidance takes the form of high absenteeism, neglect of homework and overall disengagement leading to failure. (p. 683)

This description matches Erika's positioning in the language arts classroom. She didn't hand in her work; she sat silently disengaged during class and was failing the class. She explained her low grades by saying they were low "because I was too much into my friends and just writing notes in class." And yet her disengagement was coupled with an articulated desire to do well in school. I saw this contradiction twice with Erika: once when she was talking about school and once when she discussed her future plans. In both cases, she conveyed contradictory messages. On the one hand, she seemed to want to believe in the meritocracy of schooling; that if she just tried and worked hard she would succeed in the school system and later in the larger economic structure of U.S. society. Erika said that she wanted to get better grades. "Like now I'm trying to get my grades up because I don't want to stay here in this school anymore. Yeah, I want to go to high school." On the other hand, she didn't turn in her assignments or actively participate in class.

As a learner, Erika was marginalized and disengaged from literacy learning in the classroom. Formal literacy instruction in school is usually marked by a series of literacy events. For example, I observed students in the language arts class reading sections of a text, writing answers to questions about the text, discussing these questions in class, and then handing in their written answers for homework. Each step requested by the teacher was a literacy event. For the most part, Erika did not engage in the literacy events of the language arts classroom. She usually did not hand in work or speak in class. She was not disruptive, but not engaged. In one of my classroom observations, I was struck how easily Erika blended in. The students were sitting at desks and writing answers to questions posed by the teacher. Erika was sitting with a group of girls of color and quietly writing. From a distance, it looked like she was engaged in the assigned literacy event. But on a closer look, I saw that she was not completing the assignment but, instead, was writing a note to a friend. While not disrupting the class, she was not joining the group in the literacy event and therefore not performing a literate classroom identity.

Beneath her silence in the classroom was a student with significant life experiences and interaction with texts that were not sanctioned in the school setting. Erika was not silent because she was shy; she was silent because the school had no room for her words.

ERIKA'S VOICE

Lincoln presented a methodology for working with marginalized participants in research. According to Lincoln (1993), this type of research methodology must "lean towards the constructivist, the critical, the feminist and the action oriented, and the participative" (p. 34). In particular, special attention must be taken to "seek out stories and to engage in listening both active and patient" since "sometimes it takes an extended amount of time for the silenced to seek and find their voices and frame their stories" (p. 34). With these methodological concerns in mind, against a backdrop of her silence, I watched and noted times when Erika did speak at length. Because these times were not the norm, they stood out. When she did speak, her words indicated how she saw and experienced the world. Understanding the times and topics when Erika did use her voice has significant implications for those working with marginalized and disengaged students.

The Girls Literacy Discussion Group session in which Erika talked the most over the course of the semester was the day we were reading selections about the history of how girls' bodies are portrayed in the media from Brumberg's (1997) *The Body Project: An Intimate History of American Girls.* The book stated that over time, girls have experienced menarche earlier and earlier, which led the girls to a conversation about menstrual cramps in which Tetra told the group that she was "on birth control" because her periods were "irregular and really painful." Kaliya asked the group, "When you're on birth control, you don't have your period, right?" Shortly afterward, in an unprecedented fashion, Erika dominated the group discussion for the next 20 minutes or so, sharing with the girls her knowledge of birth control, sexually transmitted diseases (STDs), and sexuality.

In this segment of group discussion, Erika was the group expert as she had never been before. Having attended what she called a "program" at a local "doctor's clinic," she informed the other girls (though not always accurately) about the patch, sterilization, IUDs, and the pill. She then offered assistance to the other girls, saying, "I could bring you those papers [from the class] if you guys want. I could show you the different things [birth control methods] that they have."

Whereas in the language arts classroom Erika was failing, here in the group she was successfully placing herself as a knowledgeable source of important information. She demonstrated the ability to take previously gained knowledge from a program lecture and texts and transfer this information to a new setting with a new audience. Erika gained the respect of her peers in this case as they listened to her information and asked extending questions. They accepted her answers until she gave false information [she said that the pill can protect you from STDs], when the other girls jumped in to work with Erika to make collective meaning around issues of contraception.

Most of Erika's life experiences, knowledge, and texts were not sanctioned in formal school settings. Her reading of the world, based on her lived experiences, had little space in the world of acceptable public school discourse. Whether it was birth control, domestic violence, gang wars, or poverty, none of these topics were seen as acceptable or value-added conversation in the middle school classroom. Erika was left to develop her literacy on her own, perform more acceptable literate positions, and stay silent about her own meaning-making of the world around her. In a formal school setting dominated by a White and middle-class culture, Erika's "reading of the world" had little currency. Therefore, in some ways, it comes as no surprise that Erika often chose to be either silent and or to perform more "acceptable" narratives.

IMPLICATIONS AND RECOMMENDATIONS

In this era of high-stakes testing, students are labeled according to their performance on standardized test scores. Although Lincoln Middle School had a portfolio assessment program whereby each student presented a collection of his or her work before 8th-grade graduation, the real deciding factor of whether a student would graduate was based on a combination of standardized test scores and grade point average. The three key participants in my research were diverse in their standardized testing scores. Tetra tested in the 90th percentile on the standardized reading test; Moniqua scored in the 80th percentile; Erika scored the lowest, in the 25th percentile. In the academic paradigm, Tetra and Moniqua were framed as successful students, while Erika was positioned as lacking sufficient literacy and at risk of being a future drop-out. I found that all of the students, even those who were labeled as struggling readers and low academic achievers, engaged in sophisticated and complex literacy practices. However, these multiple literacies did not translate into academic success.

The modes of assessing literacy that focus exclusively on reading and writing skills must be dismantled and discarded if we are to truly see the abilities of our students. Research has indicated that the focus on testing and standards rather than on the students themselves will result in disengagement and dropping out, particularly for the most marginalized students (Easton, 2008; Hacsi, 2002; Stearns & Glennie, 2006). Administrators need to step up and stand up against policies that do not serve the needs of their students. They need to recognize the intrinsic danger of such high-stakes testing as an educational practice.

Using a model of multiple literacies, we can see the complexities of the participants' experiences with multiple texts and ways of knowing. "This research [on multiple literacies] has begun to help us recognize that school-sponsored literacy is but one way of being literate in our society and around the world" (Huot et al., 2004, p. 4). In this framework, literacies take multiple forms and exist in multiple sites. The multiple literacy framework allows both students and educators to see the multiplicity, hybridity, and complexity of students' skills and knowledge.

Erika was a silent and disengaged student; however, in a small group of six girls and one woman as facilitator, Erika's voice came alive. The Girls Literacy Discussion Group functioned as a site of action research; the space created for research purposes also gave Erika a space in the school setting where she could find and use her voice. While completely silenced in the regular language arts classroom, she was able to find a place in a small group of girls. In the Girls Literacy Discussion Group, this group of six marginalized middle school girls were given a weekly space in the middle school setting to discuss issues of importance to them. This experience was a unique one for them. As Moniqua noted, "Nobody listens to you here except for Hadar. She listens to us."

In *Teaching Black Girls,* Evans-Winters (2005) advocated for such groupings. She developed an after-school program called Circle of Sisterhood specifically for African American middle school girls, focused on "topics such as teenage sexuality, media images, hygiene and health, conflict resolution and community responsibility" and integrating a literature study, interviews with woman role models, and topics based on the girls' own interests. The purpose of the group was to offer a "safe and separate space" to promote positive identity formation and build resiliency" (p. 162). Such groups can allow marginalized girls to find a voice in the school setting.

As a middle school teacher, I know that in a public school setting, a discussion group with six students is a rare occurrence. In the current economic climate with extreme budget cuts in funding for public education, middle school teachers are fighting to cap their overflowing classes let alone advocate for smaller groupings. However, the fact that such a group can help students, especially marginalized and disengaged students, speaks to the need to fight for funds for such configurations in the public middle school setting. Prevention measures like these will ultimately save money because education and empowerment are less expensive than paying future projected costs associated with disengaged students who drop out. Overall, funding for small classes in the public school system has been restricted to special education programs. There are some cases of funding for small classes for special drop-out prevention programs, but often these programs are only for high school students, often for those who have already dropped out, and often in the form of alternative schools. Middle school students like Erika who are disengaged learners would also benefit from small groups or lower student-teacher ratios. These programs need funding and support. The Girls Literacy Discussion Group contributes to the research that advocates for small discussion groups as a contribution to building resiliency for marginalized students.

Ultimately, we can't allow bad policy or current budget crises to detract from research-based pedagogy proven to be successful. At all levels, those of us in the classrooms must continue to resist high-stakes testing, higher class numbers, and cuts in programs that make a difference in the lived realities of our students.

CHAPTER 9

Girls and the Achievement Gap

The *achievement gap* is the term given to disparities in academic achievement between groups based on class or race. This achievement gap results in inequity of economic resources, earning power, and other positive life outcomes. In this research, there was an achievement gap between the most and least economically privileged participants. This research provides new insight on how the achievement gap is still being perpetuated, some of the complex issues related to the achievement gap and girls in particular, and recommendations for educators working to eliminate this gap.

ON TEEN PREGNANCY

Because there are economic consequences to teen pregnancy, it is a significant topic when looking at the economic futures of girls and young women. Teen pregnancy is the leading cause of dropping out of school for adolescent girls. Research has linked dropping out of high school with negative economic outcomes, including low wages, diminished earning power, and higher chances of unemployment (Belfield & Levin, 2007; Lavin-Loucks, 2006; Valencia, 2011). In the city where this research took place, 53% of female-headed households with children under age 5 are below the poverty level (Reynis, 2009). In the state, 54% of children in poor families have parents without a high school degree, and 84% of poor children have parents without a college education (National Center for Children in Poverty, 2009). Teen pregnancy therefore becomes an indicator of increased poverty.

Teen pregnancy was a prominent topic in the Girls Literacy Discussion Group. The girls talked at times about high school, college, and jobs, but a much more prevalent topic was pregnancy and child rearing, teen pregnancy, and teen motherhood. The girls repeatedly brought up the topic of teen pregnancy and referred on several occasions to their friends and cousins who were teen mothers. All of the participants personally knew teen mothers who had had their babies during middle school. Three of the six girls were products of teen pregnancies themselves. The topic of teen pregnancy blended both their interest in sexuality and future planning as they watched how pregnancy affected the lives of other young women they knew.

One day, one of the girls posed this question: What would you do if you found out that your teen daughter was pregnant? Kaliya stated her perspective quite passionately:

> I'd tell my kid right away, "You get pregnant, I'm going to let you take care of it." If my kid gets pregnant at an early age, not to be mean, but I'm not going to help her take care of it until she matures more. Because if she's old enough to have a kid, then she should know how to take care of a kid.
>
> I wouldn't [let her have an abortion]. I'd make my kid have her kid because she was grown enough to open her legs and get pregnant! She could have said "no." She shouldn't be having sex anyways if she's 13! I don't get it! She can come talk to me. There's birth control! I would make her have the kid. She opened her legs and I don't care what ya'll say, she should see how it feels to get pregnant and she should see how it feels to take care of a kid.

Tetra responded with an opposite position:

> If I had a daughter that got pregnant, I know, I've just heard way too many stories and had way too many cousins who have gotten pregnant and their families have said, "Well, you're the one who did this, so I'm going to make you take care of it." And their entire lives, when they did have so much potential, and just because of one stupid choice, it all went down the drain.
>
> So if I had a daughter who got pregnant before she was of age and before she graduated high school, I would help. I'd help support the kid. I would not pay full money—you're going to get a job now! And I'd help take care of the kid. I'd keep the kid at home and I'd take care of it because I'd want my daughter to get an education because I don't want my kid's life to go down the drain. I've seen way too many.

Moniqua responded by removing her future self from the problem: "Well, I wouldn't have to worry about that; I'm not having kids ever. Ever. Ever. Ever."

The topic of conversation quickly shifted to abortion, and, again, the girls voiced a range of opinions. For example, Kaliya was the strongest against abortion: "I wouldn't let my kid have an abortion because I would tell her 'Would you want me to have an abortion and you wouldn't be born?'" Kaliya continued, "But I wouldn't hit my kid if she got pregnant because she would have to suffer everything else. I'm just going to let her suffer that."

Again, Tetra was Kaliya's counterpoint. "I think it's OK to get an abortion." She then backed up to agree with Kaliya. "As long as the child is not close to being fully formed. Once that happens I feel like you're just killing someone, and I wouldn't want that to happen."

For Kaliya, the issue was more clear-cut. "Still, that wouldn't be fair. You're going to kill your kid."

I tried to intercede. "I guess it depends on whether you see it as killing or not."

Moniqua jumped in to align herself with Tetra. "I don't think it's killing because they're not really alive." In this conversation, both Erika and Angela were silent.

As a collective, the group of girls voiced multiple points of view, and the tension around this issue pulled the group in several conflicting directions. In some ways, they were no different than the general public in the United States as a whole. According to a recent Gallup poll, Americans are closely divided between those who call themselves "pro-choice" at 49% and those who call themselves "pro-life" at 45% (Saad, 2011). The topic of abortion and teen pregnancy is one that very much engages the U.S. public, as evidenced by reality TV shows such as *16 and Pregnant* and *Teen Mom*.

When we discussed teen pregnancy and abortion in the Girls Literacy Discussion Group, the two most polarized sides were Kaliya and Erika, who would keep the child if they got pregnant, and Tetra and Moniqua, who would terminate the pregnancy. Both Tetra and Moniqua prioritized their education over keeping the baby. They saw themselves as having an investment in and access to the mainstream economic system, which led them to choose abortion as a way of maintaining their personal and professional educational and career goals.

Much of the literature on teenage girls vis-à-vis pregnancy and abortion links adolescent girls who choose to have abortions and economic class (Bettie, 2003; Dodson, 1999; Sidel, 1998). According to Edin and Kefalas (2005), "Affluent youth are far more likely to terminate any given pregnancy than those raised in poor, minority or single-parent households, (p. 44–45)" Likewise, Dodson (1999) found that "what most distinguishes the behavior of low income women from that of higher income or suburban teens is that, once pregnant, they are far less likely to have abortions" (p. 110).

For middle-class girls, abortion is a way to maintain their social capital of continued schooling. Studies indicate that middle- and upper-class girls tend to see abortion as a way to maintain their investment in educational and professional goals. As Moniqua stated, "I would never be able to raise a kid when I was 15. I could never do that because I still have to go to college. I still have so much of my life ahead of me."

For working-class and poor girls with little or no access to higher education, a pregnancy does not hold the same significance of interrupting a preconceived life path. Edin and Kefalas (2005) documented how poor teenage girls in urban Philadelphia chose motherhood. They noted that "unlike their wealthier sisters, who have the chance to go to college and embark on careers—attractive possibilities that provide strong motivation to put off having children—poor young women grab eagerly at the surest source of accomplishment within their reach: becoming a mother" (p. 46). If work, education, and motherhood are possible parts of the narratives of girls' future plans and higher education is removed, then motherhood and work take precedence.

For most of the girls in the Girls Literacy Discussion Group, motherhood was part of the narratives of their future plans. However, the girls did not view motherhood as an easy path or one they were eager to assume in the near future; all of the girls talked about delaying motherhood. In addition, the girls discussed the difficulties of being a teen mother, including maybe missing the prom, having to stay home all day with the child, and missing out on social activities. Even if their professional goals were far from their academic realities, they each stated a desired career path that included college. However, having goals was not always aligned with having the ability to pursue these goals.

NARRATIVES OF THE FUTURE

I asked each of the girls where she saw herself in 5 and 10 years. Their responses were oral texts about the women they saw themselves to be or becoming in the world. In examining these narratives, it was impossible to separate their visions and dreams from the socioeconomic, racial, and cultural context of their lives. Girls are bombarded all the time by messages, some subtle and some obvious, about who they are and who they are meant to be. These texts carry meaning, a hidden curriculum, about gender, race, and class. Economic privilege, in particular, was a significant factor influencing texts about their futures. Juxtaposing Tetra and Erika highlights some of the ways in which economic privilege enables school success while poverty inhibits it.

Tetra's Future Plans

When discussing future dreams, of all of the girls in the Girls Literacy Discussion Group, Tetra was the most assertive. Her future plans revolved around her interest in music. Tetra had already taken steps to assure the success of her plans. She played several instruments, including trumpet, euphonium, trombone, and piano, and was learning guitar and violin. She participated in the honors band at school as well as the competitive city-wide youth symphony. She said that she planned to attend one of the best public high schools in the city with one of the top music programs.

In many ways, Tetra was the most privileged of the girls in the group. She was the only White student. She was also the wealthiest, which in this group meant upper middle class. She lived in a split-level home in a quiet suburban-looking neighborhood with her two parents and one older sister. Her parents, both professional educators, had summers off from work and were able to spend the time with their daughters. Of all the girls in the group, Tetra's family was the most involved in her education, from attending conferences to playing an active role in helping with class assignments and decision making. Of the key participants, she also mentioned the most educational resources at home, including several computers, video games, books, Internet access, and musical instruments.

Tetra's class privilege influenced the role of literacies in her life. Because of her economic advantages, Tetra had access to many forms of literacies that low-income students may not have access to, from private music classes and books purchased online to a house filled with modern technologies. Instead of having to work or help with household chores, Tetra had a significant amount of leisure time, which she used to read, practice her instrument, or go online.

The development of Tetra's musical literacies indicated class privilege. She practiced nearly an hour a day and took private music lessons in addition to her involvement in school music activities. Tetra planned to continue to be involved in the school music program in high school, noting that for high school band, "you have to pay like over a hundred dollars per year to be in the band." Lincoln Middle School was the feeder school to two high schools, and Tetra was scheduled to attend the school with the higher socioeconomic standing. Not coincidentally, it also had one of the best music programs in the city. In addition, Tetra played with the city's elite Youth Symphony, which she noted was class-restrictive. "It's more of a middle- and upper-class thing." The Youth Symphony also had a summer program that Tetra said "is really expensive" but a stepping-stone to success in the Youth Symphony.

From Tetra's descriptions, her family life was filled with many forms of formal and informal literacies. Her parents both liked to read, and she referred several times to literature in her home. For example, in one group discussion about whether books can change your life, she said, "My mom was just telling me last night how this book changed her life, like she thought differently after reading it." She told the group that her mom liked to read the magazine *Oprah*, listed different movies she had watched with her family, and referred to her sister's diary. Her family had an abundance of technology; Tetra reported, "In my family, everyone in my house has their own TV and DVD player."

For Tetra and her family, the computer was a central tool in their lives. "I love the computer!" she exclaimed. She said that she used her computer "every single day and on Sundays I spend the entire day on the computer." On school days she would get on for "an hour to 2 hours, depending on how nice my mommy is." Her parents were also frequent computer users. As she explained, "My mom, my dad, and my sister, we all use the computer and we all use Internet. My mom and dad *live* on e-mail." They had several computers. "We have two computers but only one works really well, and if you want to be really technical, we actually own like four or five computers, but we only have two of them up because the other two are completely worthless, and we just need to throw them in a junk pile, but my mom just won't get rid of them." The picture Tetra painted of the abundance of technology in her life and home illustrated a certain class standing, whether she was aware of it or not. In this sense, Tetra was privileged by her access to multiple forms of literacies.

In addition, as a child of educators, Tetra lived in a home culture similar to that of the school culture. Her parents knew how to navigate the educational system and help her make decisions about her education. Tetra's family discussed her educational decisions together. Tetra's sister attended high school, took honors English, and persuaded Tetra not to take the honors course. Her parents talked it over with her:

> My mom thought I should go [into honors English], but she knows that I have a problem with spelling and I'm not a very neat writer and I don't really have good grammar or anything. She said, "For those reasons, I'd say you shouldn't go.". . . Then my dad, he said, "You don't have good grammar. You don't have good spelling. You're not very good at the subject. I wouldn't do it." So the rest of my family agreed that I shouldn't go in, even though Ms. Carpenter wanted to sign me up for it.

Instead, they decided that she should go into honors algebra:

> My sister, she was talking with me, and said that right now I could probably be in an algebra class. She said that right now I'd probably have a C or a B in that. In honors algebra I might do really well in that. My entire family agrees with that, too. It's really funny—we all agree.

This example indicates how Tetra's home culture and conversations complemented her life at school. It also shows how her parents had the time and cultural capital to support Tetra in her schooling journey. They knew how to help her make academic decisions that will enable Tetra to make the most out of her engagement with the public school system.

Erika's Future Plans

In contrast to Tetra, Erika was the least privileged of the girls in terms of the social and economic capital valued in school. She was low-income, Hispanic, had previously been in special education classes, and had been held back a grade. She lived in a trailer in a poorer section of the city with her mother, her brother, and sometimes her mother's boyfriend, who was in and out of a home filled with domestic conflict. Erika's father and her brother's father had also been involved in domestic conflict with her mother. Her father had been in prison and was a local gang leader. Her mother worked as a dental assistant in town. Her mother and grandmother had been planning to attend the spring parent-teacher conference, but missed it.

When discussing her future dreams, Erika was inconsistent. In one interview she said that she had an idea of what she wanted to do after high school but couldn't "pronounce the name." After some probing, it seemed that she was referring to becoming a neonatal nurse, although in another circumstance she called it a pediatrician and then a Presbyterian.

"When I graduate high school I want to be a, what was it?" Erika started; then she paused.

"Well, describe it — what they do," I responded.

"A Presbyterian thing. That does babies and stuff," she replied

"Where did you get the idea?" I asked.

"Well, last year we were working on what we wanted to become when we get older, when we get out of high school," Erika responded. "So I was reading about a Presbyterian and I was reading about it and I was really, really interested in it. So I'm deciding to go to it."

Later in the semester I asked her a similar question. "Where do you see yourself in 10 years?" This time her answer was much different. "In bed asleep," she replied. I pictured her in bed, covers over her head, with an expression similar to the one when she lays her head down on her desk in class, the physical embodiment of disengagement.

While Erika articulated a desire to pursue a career in the medical field, she was not set up for success in this area. She had been given very little idea of the steps needed to make that decision come true. She had worked on one research project during 7th grade but was still unsure of what the job she wanted was called or how to get there. For example, here's how she described her vocational goals: "When I go to high school, I'm going to get my LTD or whatever that is for nursing. Then after that, I'm going to go to college and I'm going to get my other one." The vagueness of her answers stood in direct opposition to Tetra's clear sense of direction and assertiveness.

Unfortunately, Erika was not receiving enough support to successfully pass 8th grade, let alone make it to nursing or medical school. Erika's language arts teacher said that Erika was in jeopardy of failing 8th grade. She was failing most of her classes for most of the semester. If she did pass the 8th grade, the odds that she would leave school before earning a high school diploma were high (Lee & Burkam, 2002; Valencia, 2011). Even the language arts teacher felt that she was not doing enough to support Erika. "I don't think we're doing enough in my classroom to help kids who are really low," Ms. Carpenter admitted to me. "Like Erika should probably be reading out loud to me several times a week."

Current educational statistics indicate that Erika's chances of dropping out before she finishes high school are high. In the Lincoln Middle School district, only about 50% of students graduated from high school with their peers. The rate was even higher for students of color. Just being Latina put Erika in an at-risk category. Historically, Latinos have persistently had the highest drop-out rates among major ethnic groups (Rumberger & Rodriguez, 2011). According to the U.S. Department of Education , the high school drop-out rate for Latinas is higher than that for girls of any other race or ethnic group (Chapman, C., Laird, J., and KewalRamani, A., 2010) Nationally, there is a gap of 28 percentage points in the graduation rates of White and Hispanic girls (AAUW, 2008).

Living in poverty, as Erika did, also has a strong correlation with drop-out rates. National data show that students with families in the lowest income group are the most likely to drop out of high school, at rates more than three times those of the two highest income groups (Chapman, C., Laird, J., and KewalRamani, A., 2010). Erika had transferred from a high-poverty school district where she had been schooled most of her life. Orfield and Lee (2005) noted that there is a "strong relationship between concentrated school poverty and low achievement (p. 7). Her previous school was a high-poverty school with 75% low-income students as well as an intensely segregated school, with over 90% students of color. Orfield and Lee (2005) wrote of the educational effects of high-poverty schooling:

> [High poverty school] communities usually reflect conditions of distress— housing inadequacy and decay, weak and failing infrastructure and critical

lack of mentors and shortage of jobs—all which adversely affect [the] children's educational success . . . high poverty schools must also struggle with challenges posed by enrolling a student body lacking health and proper nutrition, violence in the form of crime and gangs and unstable home environments. (p. 15)

Erika's mother and grandmother both wanted her to do well in school. They both made extra efforts to transfer Erika and her brother to Lincoln Middle School, on the opposite side of town. Erika's mother did not want her to end up as she had—a teen mother in a low-income job. She watched over her: She would not let her be alone with her boyfriend, nor would she let her hang out at the mall or wear clothes that were too revealing. She registered her for a class at the local public health clinic so Erika could learn about birth control rather than risk teen pregnancy.

At the same time, their actions were not enough to help Erika succeed in the educational system. One day Ms. Carpenter told me that Erika's mother and grandmother were coming in for a teacher-parent conference. I waited to meet them, but they never showed up. Ms. Carpenter felt that there was a lot more that the family could and should have been doing to support Erika's education. "They should be in here for conferences, checking her homework each night, getting her tutoring," she explained. "Let's be real," she continued, "If it was my child, I'd demand an IEP [individualized education program] and demand that the school provide the services she needs to succeed."

Bettie (2003) described parents similar to Erika's family: "It is not the case that parents did not value education for their children; they clearly did. Rather, the issue is one of social and cultural capital, where working-class parents lack the social networks and skills to enable their child" (p. 82). Bettie went on to describe some of the nuances involved with the lack of "economic and cultural capital," which she described as the "weapons of class struggle":

> The fact that they don't have the money or time (because of jobs) to participate in extracurricular activities, the fact that college is unaffordable and work necessary . . . the use of nonstandard grammar, parents who cannot help with homework, who may not know about the distinction between college-prep and non-prep courses, who may not know about college entrance exams, who themselves lacked the academic skills to go to college . . . who may wrongly assume that the school will adequately educate their child without their participation, who might desire to avoid the school themselves because it is a familiar site of failure and intimidation. (p. 108)

Likewise, Erika's mother and grandmother clearly cared about Erika's educational success but were unable to match parents like Tetra's in the level of support they could provide.

Erika presented two different narratives of where she saw herself in the future. On one hand, she talked about entering the medical field. On the other hand, she presented another picture through comments like in the future she'll be "in bed asleep" or "everyone says they're never going to have kids and then it happens." These comments reflected a passivity and disengagement, parallel to Erika's relationship to school.

These two contradictory narratives about her future were linked to Erika's performance of a school-based literacy identity. The socioeconomic context is crucial to understanding her positioning with school-based literacies, as we must to examine "the hidden and obscured dimensions of literacy that have to do with culture, class, gender, race and relations of power" (Henry, 1998, p. 236). Erika's reading of the world as a low-income Hispanic girl had taught her to question whether the institutions of schooling would actually allow her to maintain a position of being a successful student. Although Erika was sometimes able to perform a middle-class identity to assimilate into the school culture, there were limitations to how much she could really perform a successful literate school identity. After all, "schools either intentionally or unintentionally support the values, beliefs and actions of some students while excluding, punishing or marginalizing others" (O'Brian, Springs, & Stith, 2001, p. 109). Erika, like other marginalized students, "[bore] the residuals of having been part of a group of people described by both achievement test and school personnel as the 'have-nots' in terms of access to cultural capital through literate means" (Alvermann, 2001, p. 680). Erika, like other marginalized students, struggled with maintaining a vision of the future that gave her access to institutions of power.

GIRLS AND THE ACHIEVEMENT GAP

Tetra and Erika were two extremes in the public school setting, both in terms of academic achievement and social and economic capital. Their privilege or lack thereof influenced which options were truly open to them and which were closed off. While college was a stated goal for all the members of the Girls Literacy Discussion Group, the reality is that entrance to college is guarded by gatekeepers and only some of these girls will actually be able to pursue that path. Studies have indicated that socioeconomic background is one of the most significant indicators of school success (Jones, 2006; Lareau, 2000; Lavin-Loucks, 2006; Lee & Burkam, 2002; Oakes, 2008; Orr, 2003). For example, recent research shows that 22% of children who have lived in poverty do not graduate from high school, compared to 6% of those who have never been poor (Hernandez, 2011). Race also plays a role in the achievement gap. Children of color are disproportionately more likely not only to live in poverty but to live in neighborhoods with concentrated poverty and low-performing schools (Hernandez, 2011). Coupled with racism, these factors contribute to the racialization of the achievement gap. Lee and Burkam (2002) noted:

> Demographic factors that are generally seen as rendering children at risk of school failure—such as single-parent family structure, lack of English usage in the household, large family size, residing in a large city or a rural area—are more common among Black and Hispanic children and their families; the frequency of these risks are also negatively related to family socioeconomic status. On the other hand, factors generally seen as advantageous for children's school progress—suburban residence, center-based child-care experience, owning children's books, being read to frequently, owning an in-home computer, and visiting the public library are more common among White and Asian children and those from higher SES families. (p. 44)

The inequality in educational opportunities and achievement begins at a young age and expands over time. Tetra began elementary school in the school where her mother was a teacher, a school in a quiet neighborhood with an excellent reputation. In contrast, Erika's experience in elementary school included moving several times and changing schools, attending at least one school that was ranked as "at risk," being placed in special education, and repeating a grade. "Social inequalities in school increase as children advance through school mainly because of differentiation in educational experiences that begin as early as first grade (with reading groups, special education placement and retention)" (Lee & Burkam, 2002, p. 7). These distinctions "extend through elementary school (as ability grouping, special education and gifted and talented programs) and are well recognized by high school (with formal and informal tracking, advanced placement and the like)" (p. 7). Although in middle school the two girls were in the same language arts class, they were tracked for math and elective courses, with Tetra in the honors math class and honors band while Erika remained in the "regular" track for both. Next year, when they begin high school, the inequality will be even greater as Erika will attend regular education classes at the lower-income and less prestigious public high school while Tetra will attend advanced and honors classes at the better-ranked high school in the "Whiter" and wealthier section of town.

Studies of queer youth like Tetra indicate that they are at risk of dropping out of school, missing school due to harassment, and committing suicide (Kosciw et al., 2010). Tetra identified as lesbian/bisexual, used her body to reflect a "butch" gender expression, and was vocal to other students at her middle school about her difference. However, she was one of the girls in the group with the highest academic achievement, the clearest future goals, and the most support to enable her academic, vocational, and personal success in the future. Tetra was harassed at school, experienced feelings of depression and loneliness, and saw herself as an "oddball" but had enough social capital and additional support to build the resiliency needed to succeed in the educational system. These tools included race and class privilege, a vast connection to many literacies including technology and music, a mother who was emotionally supportive of her sexual identity, a school setting with a Gay-Straight Alliance, and a home culture that paralleled the school culture of power.

On the other hand, Erika was at much greater risk of future academic and economic difficulties. She lived with everyday violence in her home. She did not have social capital in terms of race or class; she was Hispanic and working poor. She was barely passing 8th grade, and her future goals were blurry and unsupported. Therefore, when we look at girls and the achievement gap, we must examine all the complex layers of identity and privilege and how girls are positioned in society given this diversity.

IMPLICATIONS AND RECOMMENDATIONS

Girls are not only at higher risk than boys to be underpaid for equal work and underrepresented in positions of economic power; they are also at variable risk based on factors such as race and class. The achievement gap found between girls in school impacts their adult lives because social and economic capital and power are linked to academic achievement. This gap represents not only a discrepancy in school achievement "but a larger gap in access to positive life outcomes across multiple dimensions" (Lavin-Loucks, 2006, p. 8). The success of girls in school is intimately intertwined with all of the topics discussed in this book: multiple literacies; media and how girls see themselves; sexualities and the choices they make; violence in their everyday lives; race, class, and sexual identities; how they learn to build resiliency and use their literacies to build personal power and plan for their futures.

Taking on the issue of the achievement gap among students seems like an overwhelming task. An entire book, if not an entire library, could be devoted to this topic. As those who seek better lives for all of our students, we must be committed to addressing issues of social and economic justice in our classrooms, our schools, and the community at large. These changes include action on the macro level as well as the small steps that we as educators can take in our classrooms and our school communities. The following recommendations represent small but significant moves in this direction.

Future Planning

Many educational theorists have documented and explored how social class is reproduced; that is, how low-income students often, despite their values, desires, and even academic achievement, end up in low-income jobs; in many studies, schools are held accountable for reproducing the economic status quo (Anyon, 1997; Counts, 1932; Fine, 1991; Finn, 2009; Hicks, 2002; Weis, 1990; Willis, 1977). One way to counteract this reproduction of social capital is to give marginalized students the tools they will need to succeed in the systems of power (Delpit, 2006). Students, like Erika, who enter schools without the cultural capital needed to succeed there, need spaces to learn how to play the game. Bordieu's theory of cultural capital and reproduction rests on the idea that schools reinforce the social classes by privileging the linguistic and cultural capital held by the upper and middle classes. "Well-off families decisively consolidate their advantage by investing their cultural capital in the sections most likely to ensure it the highest and most durable academic profitability" (Bourdieu & Passeron, 1977, p. 82). Teachers can be explicit in teaching "the discourse patterns, interactional styles and spoken and written language codes that will allow them success in the larger society" (Delpit, 2006, p. 29). Explicitly teaching how to apply to colleges, what you need to succeed in a given profession, and the types of courses you need to take in middle school and high school to enable this success is a small but necessary step in working toward those larger goals.

As teachers, we have the power to help our schools implement useful programs and make sure that they are truly accessible to all students. For example, a program like Take Your Daughters to Work Day is intended to give girls like Erika access to the work world. However, at Lincoln Middle School, working-class and poor girls like Erika came to school that day because they didn't have access to sites where they could visit, while girls like Tetra went to visit a lawyer's office, arranged by a close friend of the family. This was class reproduction in action. Instead, teachers' and administrators' schools could work together to make communitywide plans that would allow all students to visit professionals in their offices.

As discussed in Chapters 5 and 9, girls need critical and open discussion around issues of sexuality. As long as teachers either resist or are forbidden to address issues of sexuality in the classroom, we are failing to help girls make plans about their futures. When it comes to the academic future of girls, teen pregnancy is a topic of significance. The potential impact that pregnancy can have on girls' educational and vocational futures is enormous compared to the impact on boys. It is crucial that all students, especially girls, have spaces to explore issues of sexuality, pregnancy, and pregnancy prevention if girls are truly to have choices in determining the direction of their lives.

In addition, lessons in critical literacy as discussed in Chapters 4 and 5 are crucial to students' understandings of the powers that be, their relationships to these systems, and ways to find themselves in this complex and interactive world. A curriculum that has critical literacy at its core will empower students to examine themselves, what role they play in maintaining the status quo, what role the status quo plays in their lives, and how to live a more successful and authentically free life. These difficult conversations will lead to a school environment that invites multiple perspectives and experiences, opening the doors for marginalized students to feel at home in the school environment. Reading together critically the texts of the hidden curriculum will reduce its power and allow students to create texts that help them succeed.

A Call to Action

Here's where teachers can make a difference, one student at a time. The focus of our efforts must be, for all students, on scaffolding and supporting their growth. As Ms. Carpenter pointed out, Erika needed more support than the school was currently providing. "I feel like [Erika] should have resource room. I feel like we should have somewhere where she can get some help, but we don't." Erika should have received and deserved to receive tutoring, counseling, additional school services, and an investigation into why an 8th-grade student was testing at a 2nd-grade level. Instead, she was left to fail. This approach is completely unacceptable and yet all too often reflects the experience of students of color and low-income students. If schools do not begin taking action for each failing student, it points to a flaw in the entire system. "If any child is left behind, the system has failed, no matter how well some may have succeeded. A system for all is implicit in its inception; it is a system for all" (Miller & Kirkland, 2010, p. 5). Erika is a symbol of a failing system.

I have taught in both public and private schools. The approach to struggling students is one of the most prominent differences I found between these two systems. In private schools, when a student is failing or demonstrating a lack of skills in a particular area, a conference is called, modifications are made, and there may be advocacy for testing or private tutoring. In short, there is a call for action. In public schools, the response is more varied, depending on the teachers and the parents. There may be a call to action or there may be no response at all or something in between.

I would argue that all the members of the Girls Literacy Discussion Group, and perhaps all students, need a call to action. Erika certainly needed a team approach that looked at all the options and all the resources available. Her teacher, Ms. Carpenter, felt that there was a lot more that the school could and should have been doing to support Erika's education. Erika is an interesting example because her mother was an active agent for change, since she purposefully transferred Erika from a high-poverty school to a more middle-class one. "Research affirms that students from poor families given a chance to attend middle-class schools do far better than students from poor families who attend high poverty schools" (Kahlenberg, 2006, p. 23). This success is attributed to elements often found at middle-class schools like Lincoln, including certified and qualified teachers, active parents, supportive peers, a safe and healthy physical environment, and adequate resources for learning. However, in Erika's case, this move at the beginning of 8th grade was not enough on its own to counter other factors at play.

As teachers and administrators, we can fill the gaps left by parents, take academic failure seriously, and make our own call for action. We can work with parents and outside resources to support each and every student to succeed. Most importantly, we must value all students as if they were our own children. We can value their work and their literacies and see their strengths, not just their deficits. As bell hooks (1994) noted, "To begin, the [teacher] must genuinely value everyone's presence (p. 8)." When we value every student, we will take action for each one.

Social Justice and Embracing Multiple Literacies

The achievement gap is bigger than No Child Left Behind, or small stop-gap measures, or looking at one student at a time. It is a complex societal problem that requires change at all levels; focusing on one factor or solution overlooks the complexity of the situation. We must work together at all levels to make schools sites for democracy, equality, and liberation. We must find ways to confront all biases from the front office, to the school textbooks, to after-school activities, to closed-ended assessments.

If we embrace "equality" as a mantra and notice and take action every time stumbling blocks get in the way of our commitment to justice, then we will instigate a shift in perspective at all levels and sites. The entire schooling system must be committed to social justice and a change in the status quo. The only way that schools have a chance at promoting equality is to de-center the White middle-class experience and truly open the door to success for all students. The efforts of teachers like Ms. Carpenter are a beginning, but a patchwork of progressive teachers is not enough. The schools need systemic change on every level.

Schools are still contributing to a reproduction of the status quo when students who enter the public educational system with social capital continue to be privileged by the system with more resources, support, and encouragement than those students with less social capital. Although in its written materials Lincoln Middle School claimed to support all students, in reality, the school privileged students who were White and middle class. This bias can be seen in several concrete ways. For example, the overwhelming majority of the teachers were White while the majority of support staff (janitors, cafeteria workers, secretaries) were people of color. Such demographics send messages to the students about academic achievement, power imbalances, and race. The special education classes had more students of color; the gifted program had a disproportionate number of White students. Less easy to document but still as real was the pervasive White middle-class culture and values that permeated areas such as curriculum, classroom conversation, and assessment.

Many of the teachers, including Ms. Carpenter, were committed to actively addressing oppression in their individual classrooms. They did this by teaching about intolerance and discrimination, by including diverse authors and subjects in their curriculum, by hosting a Gay-Straight Alliance, and by openly confronting biased behavior when they observed it.

As I've stated throughout the book, embracing multiple literacies in both the classroom curriculum and the assessment of students will also address issues of inequality and de-centering the middle-class and White experiences. When the work of marginalized students in its multiple forms is seen and valued by those determining what academic success is, more and more students will be successful at school. Right now "federal and state policies dictate what counts as literacy in high-stakes assessments in our schools," but teachers know that these traditional assessments are "too narrow, too externally driven and too divorced from everyday literacy content to capture the complexities we see every day in our programs" (Stornaiuolo, Hull, & Nelson, 2009, pp. 382–384). Teachers need the freedom to allow a multiple literacies framework to drive their curriculum, conversations, and assessments of the students in their classes.

Ultimately, as educators we must rise to the challenge of improving the educational system for marginalized students, beginning with a pedagogy of hope, to quote Paulo Freire. We must believe that change is possible in order to make change. This change begins with hearing the voices of marginalized students, like Erika, Tetra, and Moniqua, and including their perspectives and lived experiences as an integral part of the dialogue around learning and literacy education.

In conclusion, I believe it all comes down to seeing and hearing our students. What motivated this research was a desire to have time to do exactly that: to hear what my students were thinking, doing, planning, reading, writing, engaging with, and struggling with. That must be our starting place: real students in real public schools. Authentic change will begin in the classrooms, where students and teachers gather with the potential of meaningful and life-changing conversations and studies. It is in these spaces, and these spaces alone, that the future begins.

References

Alan Guttmacher Institute. (2011). *In brief: Fact sheet: Teenagers, sex and pregnancy.* Retrieved from the Alan Guttmacher Institute: http://www.guttmacher.org/pubs/FB-ATSRH.html

Allison, D. (1994). *Skin: Talking about sex, class and literature.* Ithaca, NY: Firebrand Books.

Alvermann, D. E. (2001). Reading adolescents' reading identities: Looking back to see ahead. *Journal of Adolescent & Adult Literacy, 44*(8), 676–690.

Alvermann, D. E. (2004). *Adolescents and literacies in a digital world.* New York: Peter Lang.

Alvermann, D. E. (2009). *Sociocultural constructions of adolescence and young people's lives.* In L. Christenbury, R. Bomer, & P. Smagorinsky, P. (Eds.), *Handbook of adolescent literacy research* (pp. 14–25). New York: Guilford.

Alvermann, D. E., Hinchman, K. A., Moore, D. W., Phelps, S. F., & Waff, D. R. (Eds.). (1998). *Reconceptualizing the literacies in adolescent lives.* Mahwah, NJ: Lawrence Erlbaum Associates.

Alvermann, D. E., Hinchman, K. A., Moore, D. W., Phelps, S. F., & Waff, D. R. (Eds.). (2006). *Reconceptualizing the literacies in adolescent lives* (2nd ed.). Mahwah, NJ: Lawrence Erlbaum Associates.

Alvermann, D. E., Moon, T. S., & Hagood, M. C. (1999). *Popular culture in the classroom: Teaching and researching critical media literacy.* Newark, DE: International Reading Association.

Anfara, V. A., Brown, K. M. & Mangione, T. L. (2002). Qualitative analysis on stage: Making the research process more public. *Educational Researcher, 31* (7), 28–38.

Anyon, J. (1997). *Ghetto schooling: A political economy of urban educational reform.* New York: Teachers College Press.

Anzaldúa, G., & Keating, A. (Eds.). (2002). *This bridge we call home.* New York: Routledge.

Baker, J. M. (2002). *How homophobia hurts children: Nurturing diversity at home, school and in the community.* New York: Harrington Park Press.

Barbieri, M. (1995). *Sounds from the heart: Learning to listen to girls.* Portsmouth, NH: Heinemann.

Belfield, C., & Levin, H. M. (Eds.). (2007). *The price we pay: Economic and social consequences of inadequate education.* Washington, DC: Brookings Institution Press.

Bernal, D. D., Elenas, C. A., Godinez, F. E., & Villenas, S. (Eds.). (2006). *Chicana/ Latina education in everyday life: Feminist perspective on pedagogy and epistemology.* Albany: State University of New York Press.

Bettie, J. (2003). *Women without class: Race and identity among White and Mexican-American youth.* Berkeley: University of California Press.

Bissex, G. L., & Bullock, R. H. (1987). *Seeing for ourselves: Case-study research by teachers of writing.* Portsmouth, NH: Heinemann.

Black, R. W., & Steinkuehler, C. (2009). Literacy in virtual worlds. In L. Christenbury, R. Bomer, & P. Smagorinsky (Eds.), *Handbook of adolescent literacy research* (pp. 217–287). New York: Guilford.

Blackford, H. V. (2004). *Out of this world: Why literature matters to girls.* New York: Teachers College Press.

Bloustien, G. (2003). *Girl making: A cross-cultural ethnography on the processes of growing up female.* New York: Berghahn Books.

Bornstein, K. (1994). *Gender outlaw: On men, women and the rest of us.* New York: Vintage.

Bourdieu, P., & Passeron, J. (1977). *Reproduction in education, society and culture.* Beverly Hills, CA: Sage.

Bowles, S., & Gintis, H. (1976). *Schooling in capitalist America: Educational reform and contradictions of economic life.* New York: Basic Books.

Brantlinger, E. (2003). Dividing classes: How the middle class negotiates and rationalizes school advantage. New York: RoutledgeFalmer.

Brodkin, K. (1998). *How Jews became White folk and what that says about race in American.* New Brunswick, NJ: Rutgers University Press.

Brown, L. M., & Gilligan, C. (1992). *Meeting at the crossroads.* New York: Ballantine.

Bruce, D. L. (2009). Reading and writing video: Media literacy and adolescents. In L. Christenbury, R. Bomer, & P. Smagorinsky (Eds.), *Handbook of adolescent literacy research* (pp. 287–304) New York: Guilford.

Brumberg, B. (1997). *The body project: An intimate history of American girls.* New York: Vintage.

Bruya, B., & Olwell, R. (2006). Schools that "flow." *Education Week.* 25(16), 31.

Bucholtz, M. (1999). Why be normal? Language and identity practices in a community of nerd girls. *Language in Society, 28,* 203–223.

Bucholtz, M. (2011). *White kids, language, race and styles of youth identity.* New York: Cambridge University Press.

Bureau of Justice Statistics (2005). Family violence statistics. Retrieved from the Bureau of Justice Statistics website: http://bjs.ojp.usdoj.gov/index.cfm?ty=pbdetail&iid=828

Butler, J. (1999). *Gender trouble: Feminism and the subversion of identity.* New York: Routledge.

Byrne, R. (1983). How to use technology to make you more aware and alive. Retrieved from the Center for Media Literacy website: http://www.medialit.org/reading-room/how-use-technology-make-you-more-aware-and-alive

Cahn, A., Kalagian, T., & Lyon, C. (2011). Business models for children's media. In S. L. Calvert & B. J. Wilson (Eds.), *The handbook of children, media, and development* (pp. 27–48). Malden, MA: Wiley-Blackwell.

Cammarota, J., & Romero, A. (2006). A critically compassionate intellectualism for Latina/o students: Raising voices above the silencing in our schools. *Multicultural Education, 14*(2), 16–23.

Carah, N. (2010). *Pop brands: Branding, popular music and young people.* New York: Peter Lang.

Carico, K. M. (2001). Negotiating meaning in classroom literature discussions. *Journal of Adolescent & Adult Literacy, 44*(6), 510–518.

Chandler-Olcott, K., & Mahar, D. (2003). Adolescents' anime-inspired "fanfiction": An exploration of multiliteracies. *Journal of Adolescent & Adult Literacy, 46*(7), 556–566.

Chapman, C., Laird, J., and KewalRamani, A. (2010). *Trends in High School Dropout and Completion Rates in the United States: 1972–2008* (NCES 2011-012). National Center for Education Statistics, Institute of Education Sciences, U.S. Department of Education. Washington, DC. Retrieved from National Center for Education Statistics website: http://nces.ed.gov/pubsearch/pubsinfo. asp?pubid=2011012

Charmaz, K. (2006). *Constructing grounded theory.* Thousand Oaks, CA: Sage.

Cherland, M. (1994). *Private practices: Girls reading fiction and constructing identity.* London: Taylor & Francis.

Chodorow, N. (1978). *The reproduction of mothering: Psychoanalysis and the sociology of gender* (2nd ed.). Berkeley: University of California Press.

Christenbury, L., Bomer, R., & Smagorinsky, P. (Eds.). (2009). *Handbook of adolescent literacy research.* New York: Guilford.

Cisneros, S. (1989). *The house on Mango Street.* New York: Vintage.

Clark, C. T., & Blackburn, M. V. (2009). Reading LGBT-themed literature with young people: What's possible? *English Journal, 98*(4), 25–32.

Collins, P. H. (2009). *Black feminist thought* (2nd ed.). New York: Routledge.

Cope, B., & Kalantzis, M. (2000). *Multiliteracies: Literacy learning and the design of social futures.* New York: Routledge.

Corbett, C., Hill, C, & St. Rose, A. (2008). Where the girls are: The facts about gender equity in education. Retrieved from the AAUW Educational Foundation website: http://www.aauw.org/learn/research/upload/whereGirlsAre.pdf

Corral, J. (2004). Lucy I'm home. In O. Edut (Ed.), *Body outlaws: Rewriting the rules of beauty and body image* (2nd ed.) (pp. 114–123). Seattle: Seal Press.

Counts, G. S. (1932). *Dare the school build a new social order?* Carbondale: Southern Illinois University Press.

Creswell, J. W. (2007). *Qualitative inquiry and research design: Choosing among five approaches* (2nd ed.). Thousand Oaks, CA: Sage.

Davis, K. (2010). Coming of age online: The developmental underpinnings of girls' blogs. *Journal of Adolescent Research, 25*(1), 145–171.

De Abreu, B. S. (2007). *Teaching media literacy.* New York: Neal-Schulman.

DeBlase, G. (2003). Acknowledging agency while accommodating romance: Girls negotiating meaning in literacy transactions. *Journal of Adolescent and Adult Literacy, 46*(8), 624–635.

Delpit, L. (2002). No kinda sense. In L. Delpit & J. K. Dowdy (Eds.), *The skin that we speak: Thoughts on language and culture in the classroom* (pp 31–48). New York: New York Press.

Delpit, L. (2006). *Other people's children.* New York: New Press.

Denner, J., & Guzman, B. (Eds.). (2006). *Latina girls: Voices of adolescent strength in the United States.* New York: New York University Press.

Dimitriadis, G. (2001). "In the clique": Popular culture, constructions of place and the everyday lives of urban youth. *Anthropology & Education Quarterly, 32*(1), 29–51.

Dodson, L. (1999). *Don't call us out of name: The untold lives of women and girls in poor America.* Boston: Beacon.

Driver, S. (2007). *Queer girls and popular culture: Reading, resisting and creating media.* New York: Peter Lang.

Duke, L., & Kreshel, P. (1998). Negotiating femininity: Girls in early adolescence read teen magazines. *Journal of Communication Inquiry, 22*(1), 48–70.

Durham, M. G. (1999) Girls, media and the negotiation of sexuality: A study of race, class and gender in adolescent peer groups. *Journalism and Mass Communication Quarterly, 76*(2), 193–216.

Dyson, A. H. (1999). Transforming transfer: Unruly children, contrary texts, and the persistence of the pedagogical order. *Review of Research in Education, 24*, 141–171.

Easton, L. B. (2008). *Engaging the disengaged: How schools can help struggling students succeed.* Thousand Oaks, CA: Corwin.

Edin, K., & Kefalas, M. (2005). *Promises I can keep: Why poor women put motherhood before marriage.* Berkeley: University of California Press.

Edut, O. (Ed.). (1998). *Adios Barbie: Young women write about body image and identity.* Seattle: Seal Press.

Edut, O. (Ed.). (2003). *Body outlaws: Rewriting the rules of beauty and body image.* Emeryville, CA: Seal Press.

Eglash, R. (2002). Race, sex and nerds: From Black geeks to Asian-American hipsters. *Social Text, 20*(2), 49–64.

Elkind, D. (1981). *Children and adolescents: Interpretive essays on Jean Piaget* (3rd ed.). New York: Oxford University Press.

Erikson, E. (1968). *Identity, youth and crisis.* New York: Norton.

Evans, G. (1988). "Those loud black girls." In Spencer, D. & Sarah, E. *Learning to Lose: Sexism and Education.* London: The Women's Press.

Evans-Winters, V. E. (2005). *Teaching Black girls: Resiliency in urban classrooms.* New York: Peter Lang.

Farmer, L. (2008). *Teen girls and technology: What's the problem, what's the solution.*

New York: Teachers College Press.

Fata, S., & Rafii, R. (2003). *Iran census report.* Washington, DC: National Iranian American Council.

Fausto-Sterling, A. (2000). *Sexing the body: Gender politics and the construction of sexuality.* New York: Basic Books.

Feistritzer, C. E., Griffin, S., & Linnajarvi, A. (2011). *Profile of teachers in the U.S. 2011.* Washington DC: National Center for Education Information. Retrieved from the National Center for Education Information website: http://www.ncei. com/Profile_Teachers_US_2011.pdf

Finders, M. (1997). *Just girls: Hidden literacies and life in junior high.* New York: Teachers College Press.

Fine, M. (1991). *Framing dropouts.* Albany: State University of New York Press.

Fine, M. (1992). *Disruptive voices: The possibilities of feminist research.* Ann Arbor: University of Michigan Press.

Fine, M., & Weis, L. (2003). *Silenced voices and extraordinary conversations: Re-imagining schools.* New York: Teachers College Press.

Finn, P. J. (1999). *Literacy with attitude: Educating working class children in their own self-interest.* Albany: State University of New York Press.

Finn, P. J. (2009). *Literacy with attitude: Educating working class children in their own self-interest* (2nd ed.). Albany: State University of New York Press.

Fleishman, P. (1997). *Seedfolks.* New York: Harper Trophy.

Fordham, S. (1996). Blacked out: Dilemmas of race, identity and success at Capital High. Chicago: University of Chicago Press.

Fordham, S. (1997). "Those loud Black girls": (Black) women, silence and gender "passing" in the academy. In M. Seller & L. Weis (Eds.), *Beyond black and white: New faces and voices in U.S. schools* (pp. 81–111). Albany: State University of New York Press.

Fordham, S., & Ogbu, J. (1986). Black students' school success: Coping with the "burden of acting White." *The Urban Review, 18*(3), 176–206.

Franzak, J., & Noll, E. (2006). Monstrous acts: Problematizing violence in young adult literature. *Journal of Adolescent & Adult Literacy, 49*(8), 662–672.

Freire, P. (1993). *Pedagogy of the oppressed.* New York: Continuum.

Freire, P., & Macedo, D. (1987). *Literacy: Reading the word and the world.* Westport, CT.: Bergin & Garvey.

Gee, J. P. (1989). Literacy, discourse, and linguistics: Introduction. *Journal of Education, 171*(1), 5–25.

Gee, J. P. (2000). Teenagers in new times: A new literacy studies perspective. *Journal of Adolescent & Adult Literacy, 43*(5), 412-420.

Gilbert, D. (1998). *The American class structure: In an age of growing inequality* (5th ed.). New York: Wadsworth Publishing Company.

Gilbert, P., & Taylor, S. (1991). *Fashioning the feminine: Girls, popular culture and schooling.* North Sydney, Australia: Allen & Unwin.

Gill, R. (2007). *Gender and the media.* Malden, MA: Polity Press.

Gilligan, C., Lyons, N., & Hanmer, T. (1990). *Making connections: The relational worlds of adolescent girls at Emma Willard School.* Cambridge, MA: Harvard University Press.

Giroux, H. A. (1998). *Channel surfing: Racism, the media and the destruction of today's youth.* New York: St. Martin's Griffin.

Hacsi, T. A. (2002). *Children as pawns: The politics of educational reform.* Cambridge, MA: Harvard University Press.

Hagood, M. C. (2002) Critical literacy for whom? *Reading Research and Instruction, 40*(3), 247–266.

Hagood, M. C. (Ed.). (2009). *New literacies practices.* New York: Peter Lang.

Haiken, M. L. (2002). Sharing "knowledge about life": Empowering adolescent girls through groups. *Voice of Youth Advocates, 24*(6), 411–416.

Halberstam, J. (1998). *Female masculinity.* Durham, NC: Duke University Press.

Hall, H. (2011). *Understanding teenage girls: Culture, identity and schooling.* New York: Rowman & Littlefield.

Havigvurst, R. J. & Taba, H. (1949). *Adolescent character and personality.* New York: Wiley.

Heath, S. B. (1984) *Ways with words.* New York: Cambridge University Press.

Hegewisch, A., Liepmann, H., Hayes, J., & Hartmann, H. (2010). Briefing paper: Separate and not equal? Gender segregation in the labor market and the gender wage gap. Retrieved from the Institute for Women's Policy Research website: www.iwpr.org

Hegewisch, A. & Williams, C. (2010) Fact sheet: The gender wage gap: 2010. Retrieved from the Institute for Women's Policy Research website: http://www.iwpr.org/publications/pubs/the-gender-wage-gap-2010

Helms, J. E. (Eds.). (1990). *Black and white racial identity: Theory, research and practice.* Westport, CT: Greenwood.

Henry, A. (1998). "Speaking up" and "speaking out": Examining "voice" in a reading/writing program with adolescent African Caribbean girls. *Journal of Literacy Research, 30*(2), 233–252.

Hernandez, D. J. (2011). *Double jeopardy: How third-grade reading skills and poverty influence high school graduation.* Retrieved from the Annie E. Casey Foundation website: http://www.aecf.org/~/media/Pubs/Topics/Education/Other/DoubleJeopardyHowThirdGradeReadingSkillsandPovery/DoubleJeopardyReport040511FINAL.pdf

Hernandez, D., & Rehman, B. (Eds.). (2002*). Colonize this! Young women of color on today's feminism.* New York: Seal Press.

Hicks, D. (2002). *Reading lives: Working class children and literacy learning.* New York: Teachers College Press.

hooks, b. (1989). *Talking back: Thinking feminist, thinking black.* Boston: South End Press.

hooks, b. (1994). *Teaching to transgress: Education as the practice of freedom.* New York: Routledge.

Horsford, S. D. (2011). *Learning in a burning house: Educational inequality, ideology and (dis)integration.* New York: Teachers College Press.

Horvitz, L. (Ed.). (2011). *Queer girls in class: Lesbian teachers and students tell their classroom stories.* New York: Peter Lang.

Huot, B., Stroble, B., & Bazerman, C. (Eds.). (2004). *Multiple literacies for the 21st century.* Cresskill, NJ: Hampton Press.

Hurtado, A. (2003). *Voicing Chicana feminisms: Young women speak out on sexuality and identity.* New York: New York University Press.

Institute for Women's Policy Research, www.iwpr.org. Retrieved November 22, 2010.

Jacob, M. (2003) My brown face. In O. Edut (Ed.), *Body outlaws: Rewriting the rules of beauty and body image* (pp. 3–13). Seattle: Seal Press.

Jones, S. (2006). *Girls, social class and literacy: What teachers can do to make a difference.* Portsmouth, NH: Heinemann.

Kahlenberg, R. D. (2006). The new integration. *Educational Leadership, 63*(8), 22–26.

Kaplan, E. B. & Cole, L. (2000). "'I want to read stuff on boys': White, Latina, and Black girls reading *Seventeen* magazine and encountering adolescence. *Adolescence, 38,* 141–158.

Kelly, M. M. (2001). "The educationa of African American youth: Literacy practices and identity representation in church and school." In E. B. Moje & D. C. O'Brian (Eds.) *Constructions of literacy: Studies of teaching and learning in and out of secondary schools.* (pp. 239–262). Mahwah NJ: Lawrence Erlbaum Associates.

Kelly, S. P. (2008). Social class and tracking within schools. In L. Weis (Ed.), *The way class works* (pp. 210–224). New York: Routledge.

Knobel, M., & Lankshear, C. (Eds.). (2007). *A new literacies sampler.* New York: Peter Lang.

Kosciw, J. G., Greytak, E. A., Diaz, E. M., & Bartkiewicz, M. J. (2010). The 2009 National School Climate Survey: The experiences of lesbian, gay, bisexual and transgender youth in our nations' schools. (GLSEN Report 2624). New York: Gay, Lesbian and Straight Education Network.

Ladson-Billings, G. J. (1995). Toward a theory of culturally relevant pedagogy. *American Education Research Journal, 35,* 465–491.

Lareau, A. (2000). *Home advantage: Social class and parental intervention in elementary education* (2nd ed.). New York: Rowman & Littlefield.

Lareau, A. (2005). *Unequal childhoods: Class, race, and family life.* Berkeley: University of California Press.

Lareau, A. (2008). Watching, waiting and deciding when to intervene: Race, class and the transmission of advantage. In L. Weis (Ed.), *The way class works* (pp. 117–133). New York: Routledge.

Lavin-Loucks, D. (2006) *The academic achievement gap.* J. McDonald Williams Institute. Retrieved March 4 2011 from www.thewilliamsinstitute.org

Lawrence-Lightfoot, S., & Davis, J. H. (1997). *The art and science of portraiture.* San Francisco: Jossey-Bass.

Leadbeater, B. J. R., & Way, N. (Eds.). (2007). *Urban girls: Resisting stereotypes, creating identities.* New York: New York University Press.

Lee, V. E., & Burkam, D. T. (2002). *Inequality and the starting gate: Social background differences in achievement as children begin school.* Washington, DC: Economic Policy Institute.

Lesko, N. (2001). *Act your age! A cultural construction of adolescence.* New York: Routledge Falmer.

Lewis, C., & Del Valle, A. (2009). Literacy and identity: Implications for research and practice. In L. Christenbury, R. Bomer, & P. Smagorinsky (Eds.), *Handbook of adolescent literacy research* (pp. 307–322). New York: Guilford.

Lewis, C., Enciso, P., & Moje, E. B. (2007). *Reframing sociocultural research on literacy identity, agency and power.* Mahwah, NJ: Erlbaum.

Lewis, C., & Fabo, B. (2005). Instant messaging, literacies and social identities. *Reading Research Quarterly, 40*(4), 470–501.

Lewison, M., Flint, A. S., & Van Sluys, K. (2002). Taking on critical literacy: The journey of newcomers and novices. *Language Arts, 79*(5), 385–392.

Lincoln, Y. S. (1993). I and thou: Method, voice, and roles in research with the silenced. In D. McLaughlin & W. B. Tierney (Eds.), *Naming silences lives: Personal narratives and the process of educational change* (pp. 29–47). New York: Routledge.

Lloyd, C. V. (1998). Adolescent girls: Constructing and doing literacy, constructing and doing gender. *Reading Research Quarterly, 33*(1), 129–136.

Lopez, N. (2003). *Hopeful girls, troubled boys: Race and gender disparity in urban education.* New York: Routledge.

Lorde, A. (1984). *Sister outsider.* Trumansberg, NY: The Crossing Press.

Lutrell, W. (2003). *Pregnant bodies, fertile minds: Gender, race and the schooling of pregnant teens.* New York: Routledge.

Madriz, E. (2000). Focus groups in feminist research. In N. K Denzin & Y. S. Lincoln (Eds.), *Handbook of qualitative research* (2nd ed., pp. 835–850). Thousand Oaks, CA: Sage.

Mahiri, J. (2001). Pop culture pedagogy and the end(s) of school. *Journal of Adolescent & Adult Literacy, 44*(4), 382–385.

Mahiri, J. (Ed.). (2004). *What they don't learn in school: Literacy in the lives of urban youth.* New York: Peter Lang.

Maier, K. S., Ford, T. G., & Schneider, B. (2008). Are middle class families advantaging their children? In L. Weis (Ed.), *The way class works* (pp. 134–148). New York: Routledge.

Mazzarella, S., & Pecora, N. O. (Eds.). (1999). *Growing up girls: Popular culture and the construction of identity.* New York: Peter Lang.

Mazzarella, S. (Ed.). (2010). *Girl wide web 2.0: Girls, Internet and the negotiation of identity.* New York: Peter Lang.

McRobbie, A. (2000). *Feminism and youth culture* (2nd ed.). New York: Routledge.

Millard, E. (1997). Differently literate: Boys, girls and the schooling of literacy. Washington. DC: Falmer.

Miller, S. J., & Kirkland, D. E. (Eds.). (2010). *Change matters: Critical essays on moving social justice research from theory to policy.* New York: Peter Lang.

Moje, E. B. (2002). Reframing adolescent literacy research for new times: Studying youth as a resource. *Reading Research and Instruction, 31*(3), 211–228.

Moje, E. B., Dillon, E. R., & O'Brian, D. (2000). Re-examining roles of learner, text, and context in secondary literacy. *The Journal of Educational Research, 93*(3), 165–180.

Moje, E. B., Willes, D. J., & Fassio, K. (2001). Constructing and negotiating literacy in the writer's workshop: Literacy teaching and learning in seventh grade. In E. B. Moje & D. G. O'Brian (Eds.), *Constructions of literacy: Studies of teaching and learning in and out of secondary schools* (pp. 193–212). Mahwah, NJ: Erlbaum.

Moore, D. W., Alvermann, D. E., & Hinchman, K. A. (Eds.). (2000). *Struggling adolescent readers: A collection of teaching strategies.* Newark, DE.: International Reading Association.

Morrison, C. (2010). *Who do they think they are? Teenage girls and their avatars in spaces of social online communication.* New York: Peter Lang.

Narayan, U. (1997). *Dislocating cultures: Identities, traditions and third world feminisms.* New York: Routledge.

National Center for Children in Poverty. (2009).www.nccp.org. Retrieved March 04, 2011.

National Foundation of Women Legislators, 2011. Facts about women legislators. Retrieved from the National Foundation for Women Legislators website: http://www.womenlegislators.org/women-legislator-facts.php

Newman, B. M., & Newman, P. R. (1986). *Adolescent development.* Columbus, OH: Merrill.

Oakes, J. (2005). *Keeping track: How schools structure inequalities* (2nd ed.) New Haven, CT: Yale University Press.

Oakes, J. (2008). Keeping track: Structuring equality and inequality in an era of accountability. *Teachers College Record, 110*(3), 700–712.

Obama, B. (2009). National information literacy awareness month proclamation. [Press release]. Retrieved from The White House Press website: http://www.whitehouse.gov/the_press_office/Presidential-Proclamation-National-Information-Literacy-Awareness-Month.

Obidah, J. E. (1998). Black-mystory: Literate currency in everyday schooling. In D. E. Alvermann, K. A. Hinchman, D. W. Moore, S. F. Phelps, & D.R. Waff (Eds.), *Reconceptualizing the literacies in adolescents' lives* (pp. 51–72). Mahwah, NJ: Erlbaum.

O'Brian, D. (2006). "Struggling" adolescents' engagement in multimediating: Countering the institutional construction of incompetence. In D. E. Alvermann, K. A. Hinchman, D. W. Moore, S. F. Phelps, & D. R. Waff (Eds.), *Reconceptualizing the literacies in adolescents' lives* (pp. 29-45). Mahwah, NJ: Lawrence Erlbaum

O'Brian, D. G., Moje, E. B., & Stewart, R. A. (2001). Exploring the contexts of secondary literacy: Literacy in people's everyday school lives. In E. B. Moje & D. G. O'Brian (Eds.), *Constructions of literacy: Studies of teaching and learning in and out of secondary schools* (pp. 27-48). Mahwah, NJ: Erlbaum.

O'Brian, D. G., Springs, R., & Stith, D. (2001). Engaging at-risk students: Literacy learning in a high school literacy lab. In E. B. Moje & D. G. O'Brian (Eds.). *Constructions of literacy: Studies of teaching and learning in and out of secondary schools* (pp. 105-123). Mahwah, NJ: Erlbaum.

Ogbu, J. (1991). Cultural diversity and school experience. In C. E. Walsh (Ed.), *Literacy as praxis* (pp. 25-50). Norwood, NM: Ablex.

Oliver, K. (1999). Adolescent girls' body narratives: Learning to desire and create a "fashionable" image. *Teachers College Record, 101*(2), 220-246.

Oliver, K. L., & Lalik, R. (2000). *Bodily knowledge: Learning about equity and justice with adolescent girls.* New York: Peter Lang.

Omi, M., & Winant, H. (1994). *Racial formation in the United States* (2nd ed.). New York: Routledge.

Orfield, G., & Lee, C. (2005). *Why segregation matters: Poverty and educational inequity.* Cambridge, MA: The Civil Rights Project, Harvard University.

Orr, A. J. (2003). Black-White differences in achievement: The importance of wealth. *Sociology of Education, 76*, 281-304.

Payne, E. C., & Smith, M (2011). The reduction of stigma in shools: A new professional development model for empowering educators to support LGBTQ students. *Journal of LGBT Youth, 8*(2), 174-200.

Payne, K. (2002). Whores and bitches who sleep with women. In C. B. Rose & A. Camilleri (Eds.), *Brazen femme: Queering femininity.* Vancouver, Canada: Arsenal Pulp Press.

Potter, W. J. (2004). *Theory of media literacy: A cognitive approach.* Thousand Oaks, CA.: Sage.

Reynis, L. (2009). Status of the economy: US, New Mexico. Bureau of Business and Economic Research. Retrieved from www.lwvabc.org/reports.

Rich, A. (1979). *On lies, secrets and silence: Selected prose 1966-1978.* New York: Norton.

Richardson, L. (1994).Writing: A method of inquiry. In N. K. Denzin & Y. S. Lincoln (Eds.). *Handbook of qualitative research* (2nd ed.). (pp. 923-948). Thousand Oaks, CA: Sage Publications.

Romero, R. M. (2007). Learning to act: Interactive performance and preservice teacher education. In P. Finn & M. E. Finn (Eds.), *Teacher education with an attitude* (pp. 95–107). Albany: State University of New York Press.

Rosenblatt, L. (1994). *The reader, the text, the poem: The transactional theory of literary work*. Carbondale: Southern Illinois Press.

Rumberger, R. W., & Rodriguez, G. M. (2011). Chicano dropouts. In R. R. Valencia (Ed.), *Chicano school failure and success* (3rd ed., pp. 76–98). New York: Routledge.

Saad, L. (2011). American still split along "pro-choice," "pro-life" lines. Gallup poll. Retrieved from the Gallup website: http://www.gallup.com/poll/147734/Americans-Split-Along-Pro-Choice-Pro-Life-Lines.aspx

Satz, M. (1997). Returning to one's house: An interview with Sandra Cisneros. *Southwest Review, 82*, 166–185.

Scribner, S. & Cole, M. (1981). *The psychology of literacy*. Cambridge, MA: Harvard University Press.

Sears, J. T. (Ed.). (2005). *Gay, lesbian, bisexual and transgender issues in educational programs, policies and practices*. New York: Harrington Park Press.

Shenk, D. (1997). *Data smog: Surviving the information gut*. New York: HarperCollins.

Sidel, R. (1998). *Keeping women and children last: America's war on the poor*. New York: Penguin.

Sizer, T. R., & Sizer, N. F. (1999). *The students are watching: Schools and the moral contract*. Boston: Beacon.

Skinner, E. N., & Licktenstein, M. J. (2009). Digital storytelling is not the new PowerPoint: Adolescents' critical constructions of presidential election issues. In M. C. Hagood (Ed.), *New literacies practices* (pp. 91–112). New York: Peter Lang.

Sprague, M. M. & Keeling, K. K. (2007). *Discovering their voices: Engaging adolescent girls with young adult literature*. Newark, DE: International Reading Association.

Stearns. E., & Glennie, E. J. (2006). When and why dropouts leave high school. *Youth and Society, 38*(1), 29–57.

Stokes, C. E. (2010). *"Get on my level": How Black American adolescent girls construct identity and negotiate sexuality on the Internet*. New York: Peter Lang.

Stornaiuolo, A., Hull, G. A., & Nelson, M. E. (2009). Mobile texts and migrant audiences: Rethinking literacy and assessment in a new media age. *Language Arts, 86*(5), 382–392.

Street, B.V. (1984). *Literacy in theory and practice*. Cambridge, UK: Cambridge University Press.

Tatum, B. D. (2003). *"Why are all the Black kids sitting together in the cafeteria?" and other conversations about race* (2nd ed.). New York: Basic Books.

Tolman, D. L. (2005). *Dilemmas of desire: Teenage girls talk about sexuality*. Cambridge, MA: Harvard University Press.

Torres, E. E. (2003). *Chicana without apology*. New York: Routledge.

U.S. Department of Health and Human Services (2011). www.hhs.gov. Retrieved October 13, 2011.

U.S. Department of Labor. (2011). www.dol.gov. Retrieved October 10, 2011.

Valencia. R. R. (2011). *Chicano school failure and success* (3rd ed.). New York: Routledge.

Walker, R. (2003). Forward. In O. Edut (Ed.), *Body outlaws: Rewriting the rules of beauty and body image* (pp. xi–xvii). Seattle: Seal Press.

Walkerdine, V., Lucey H., & Melody, J. (2001) *Growing up girl: Psychosocial explorations of gender and class.* New York: New York University Press.

Warburten, J. (2010). Me/her/Draco Malfoy: Fangirl communities and their fictions. In S. R. Mazzarella (Ed.), *Girl wide web 2.0* (pp. 117–137). New York: Peter Lang.

Weis, L. (1990). *Without work: High school students in a de-industrializing America.* New York: Routledge.

Weis, L. (Ed.). (2008). *The way class works: Readings on school, family and the economy.* New York: Routledge.

Weis, L., & Carbonell-Medina, D. (2003). Learning to speak out in an abstinence-based sex education group: Gender and race work in an urban magnet school. In M. Fine & L. Weis (Eds.), *Silenced voices and extraordinary conversations* (pp. 133–165). New York: Teachers College Press.

Weis, L., & Fine, M. (Eds.). (2005). *Beyond silenced voices: Class, race and gender in U.S. schools* (rev. ed.). Albany: State University of New York Press.

Wells, A. S., & Oakes, J. (1996). Potential pitfalls of systemic reform: Early lessons from research on detracking. *Sociology of Education (extra issue)*, 135–143.

Wilkinson, L., & Pearson, J. (2009). School culture and the well-being of same-sex attracted youth. *Gender & Society, 23*(4), 542–567.

Willis, P. (1977). *Learning to labor: How working class kids get working class jobs.* New York: Columbia University Press.

Winn, M. T. (2011). *Girl time: Literacy, justice and the school-to-prison pipeline.* New York: Teachers College Press.

Wolf, N. (1997). *Promiscuities: The secret struggle for womanhood.* New York: Random House.

Woog, D. (1995). *School's out: The impact of gay and lesbian issues on America's schools.* Los Angeles: Alyson Publications.

Young, J. P. (2001). Displaying practices of masculinity: Critical literacy and social contexts. *Journal of Adolescent & Adult Literacy, 45*(1), 4–14.

Index

Abortion, 26, 56, 71, 72, 109–111
Abstinence education, 59, 61, 71
Academic achievement
achievement gap as discrepancy in, 119; body as text and, 37, 39, 40; characteristics of student-participants and, 10; definition of, 2; future plans and, 4, 119; gender and, 2; multiple literacies and, 105–107; of nerd girls, 39; parents impact on, 116; race and, 22, 40; and role of literacies in self-understanding, 3; social justice and, 123; socioeconomic class and, 24, 115, 116. *See also specific student-participant*
Achievement gap
complexity of, 122; definition of, 108; future plans and, 6, 111–117, 119, 120–121; implications and recommendations; about, 108, 119–124; importance of, 119; and open discussions of controversial topics, 81; race and, 118; socioeconomic class and, 108, 117–118; teen pregnancy and, 108–111
Administrators, 55, 83, 106, 120–121
Adolescence
adult connections with, 19; characteristics of, 19–20, 49; diversity in, 21; myths of, 19–20; stereotypes of, 19–20; theories about, 20; understanding, 19–20
Adults
adolescent connections with, 19; hypocrisy of, 61; open discussions about

sexuality with, 69–73. *See also* Administrators; Mother(s); Parents; Teachers
Allison, Dorothy, 26
Alvermann, D. E., 15, 16, 17, 19, 43, 55, 81, 83, 94, 102, 103, 117
American Association of University Women (AAUW), 115
Anfara, V. A., 14
Angela (student-participant)
academic achievement and, 9; body image and, 52–53; body as text and, 29; characteristics of, 9; critical literacy and, 44, 45, 46, 47–48, 52–53; gender issues and, 44, 45, 46, 47–48; Internet usage by, 85, 86; invisible codes and, 28; mother/family of, 9, 65, 85; race and, 9, 29; sexuality and, 59, 60, 65; silence of, 110; social groups for, 28; socioeconomic class of, 9; teen magazines and, 44, 45, 46, 47–48; teen pregnancy and, 110; voice of, 9
Anyon, J., 19, 24, 120
Anzaldua, G., 23, 26, 30, 96
Assessment, 99, 100, 105–107, 123

Baker, J. M., 26
Barbieri, M., 19
Bartkiewicz, M. J., 26, 86, 87, 119
Bazerman, C., 10, 15, 101, 106
Beauty, 44, 52
Behavior: policing and monitoring of, 65–69
Belfield, C., 108
Belonging, 17, 23, 27, 28, 29, 91, 92. *See also* Oppositional identity
Bernal, D. D., 22, 23

Bettie, J., 12, 21–22, 23, 24, 25, 26, 34, 46, 110, 116
Birth control, 62, 64, 65, 71–72, 104, 116
Bissex, G. L., 3
Black, R. W., 85, 89
Blackburn, M. V., 71
Blackford, H. V., 27
Bloustein, G., 17, 26, 51, 68, 91, 92
Body
adornment of, 17; control of, 68; creation of own texts and, 93, 96; critical literacy and, 44, 51–53; definition of language practices and, 17; gender and, 44, 51–53; image of, 44, 51–53; plastic surgery and, 52–53; policing of girls, 52, race and, 5, 28–32; as sexual agent, 17; socioeconomic class and, 5, 28–29, 32–36, 41–42; as text, 5, 17, 28–41, 68, 96; youth culture and, 52. *See also specific student-participant*
Bomer, R., 43
Books, 3, 27, 57, 112–113
Bornstein, K., 21
Bourdieu, P., 24, 120
Bowles, S., 24
Boys/men
comparison of girls/women with, 2; critical media literacy for text saturation and, 50–51; policing and monitoring of, 68–69; sex discussions between girls and, 61–63. *See also* Gender; Masculinity
Brand names/stores, 46–47, 48
Brantlinger, E., 22, 24, 40
Brodkin, K., 21
Brown, K. M., 14, 20
Bruce, D. L., 43
Brumberg, B., 64, 104
Bruya, B., 80–81

About the Author

Hadar Dubowsky Ma'ayan is a public middle school teacher, educational researcher, and writer. She has taught courses in education at the University of New Mexico, where she earned her PhD in Language, Literacy, and Sociocultural Studies. She also studied at Bank Street College of Education, focusing on early adolescent development. She has published numerous articles in the fields of education and gender studies. Her research focuses on middle school students and issues of power and privilege, especially the intersections of class, race, gender, gender expression, and sexuality.